THE REAL ESTATE GAME PLAN

BY PAUL HOLUB

A STEP-BY-STEP STRATEGY
TO SELL YOUR HOME
FOR MAX PROFIT

Copyright © 2018 by Paul Holub

All rights reserved. This book or any portion thereof may not be reproduced or used in any manner whatsoever without the express written permission of the publisher except for the use of brief quotations in a book review.

Printed in the United States of America

Set in Sentinel by H&FJ
Designed by Aaron Wegenka

First Printing, 2018

ISBN for print
978-1732549005

ISBN for ebook
978-1-7325490-1-2

To Lauren, my amazing bride.
You inspire me daily to be a better man and achieve our dreams.
I love walking through life with you.

To Hannah and Henry,
I love you more than you will ever know.

For all who are embarking on a real estate journey of your own, that my simple babblings help you to achieve your goals.

CONTENTS

1 • **WHAT'S IT WORTH TO YOU?** Step 1: Meet with the Professional

2 • **PREPARE YOUR HOUSE & PLAN TO WIN** Step 2: De-Clutter & De-Personalize

3 • **HOMEWORK** Step 3: Do Necessary Repairs & Updates

4 • **PRETTY HOUSES SELL** Step 4: Stage the house to get it in the best shape

5 • **AMAZING PROPERTY SHOTS** Step 5: Professional Photography & Virtual Tours

6 • **STAND OUT FROM THE COMPETITION** Step 6: What Makes Your Home Unique?

7 • **THE PRICE IS RIGHT** Step 7: Pricing Your House

8 • **PETS, LAUNDRY & KIDDOS** Step 8: Make Your Home Available

9 • **MARKET LIKE CRAZY** Step 9: Get the Word Out

10 • **THE PROCESS** Step 10: Accept the Right Offer

11 • **THE WRAP UP** "That's All Folks"

• **REFERENCES & RESOURCES**

INTRODUCTION

F RUSTRATION HAD BEEN BUILDING after months on the market, with few showings and no offers. Bob and Lyn had been trying to sell their house for half a year with no luck. Some of it had to do with the local Real Estate Market, but most of their lack of success had to do with their home itself. They had a beautiful traditional home in a great neighborhood, zoned to wonderful schools. However, the house had not been cosmetically upgraded. Being built in the early 1990's this posed a challenge. When I met with them to discuss their home and a possible selling strategy, I gave them their two options; update your home or drop the price.

Upon reflection, Bob and Lyn decided to update their house. They started by removing the original laminate countertops and replacing them with a popular granite countertop and color scheme. They removed the backsplash and installed a simple travertine tile as well as updating the flooring to a 20x20" porcelain tile with a neutral design. Along with those updates, the homeowners painted the entire downstairs area and worked with a stager to ensure their newly updated house would be more visually appealing. All in all, they spent about $12,000 in improvements to their house in just under a month.

Next, it was time for my team and I to jump in. I brought in a professional photographer who took eye-catching photos. I selected the best images and then used these high-resolution pictures of their house to showcase it on our local MLS as well as all other major online real estate platforms. In addition to this, I did other forms of marketing including direct mail, Facebook ads, and an Open House. I also chose to target specific agents that often buy and sell in the area, with hopes that they might have a buyer interested in the house.

When it was all said and done, together with Bob & Lyn, we listed their house, negotiated, and accepted an offer in just over two weeks! While it was a lot of work, Bob and Lyn ended up netting an extra $15,000 above the $12,000 they spent and were extremely happy.

So, what is the extra effort worth to *you?*

I have had many clients like Bob and Lyn, they are not alone. I wrote this book because it pained me to see homeowners selling their homes and settling for less. Knowing that if they had just done a few, "correcting" alterations, they would have received a higher sales value for their home. By the time many homeowners call to list their home, they have usually done all the repairs and updates they have planned (or can afford) and are left to give me instructions to sell it "as is."

I kept thinking to myself, *"If only the homeowner knew what I know, then they wouldn't have to settle."* So, I decided to write this book. To give you a step-by-step game plan for maximizing the sale of your home.

Make no mistake, it takes work to sell your house for the top asking price, but if you are open to learning and following the steps in this book, then you can do it.

In this book, you will find all the information you need to net an additional 1%, 3%, 5% or more on the sale of your home. I will review each step of the home selling process and provide tips and tricks for preparing your house for sale, ways to professionally market, as well as renovations and updates to tackle and which ones to stay away from. And that is just the beginning.

The chapters in this book are in sequential order with each step setting you up to win. However, feel free to turn to any chapter for a quick reference. Chapter 9 on marketing and chapter 10 on the normal process of selling a house, are in my opinion, invaluable to your success. There are also some wonderful support items in the "Resource" section at the back of this book. Turn to page153 to get the list of "The Best Inexpensive Updates & Repairs to Do Prior to Selling Your Home" and an example "Real Estate Game Plan Marketing Calendar.".

Just about anyone can get more out of selling their house. Make no mistake, it is a competition out there and we need to create a winning game plan if you are going to succeed.

So, I ask again, what's it worth to you? It's a tremendous amount of work preparing your home for sale, and to get it in its best condition. Discovering what level of preparation you need is the first step. So, it is time to let the professionals in and get to work.

A WORD ON RESULTS

Even if you do all of the steps in the game plan, your house may not sell for what you are hoping for. I cannot guarantee your return on investment, just provide a game plan to hopefully get you there. That is why, having the right professionals to provide an honest outlook of your house is so critical. The other item that severely limits what you will be able to sell your house for is the appraiser. If an appraiser cannot find good comparables, then there is no way your house will appraise for the value the buyer has offered (an appraisal is required on all conforming loans, ex: Conventional, FHA, and VA). If your house doesn't appraise for the value of the loan, then the buyer will not be able to get their loan approved to fund and in turn purchase your house.

Now time for the "Official Disclaimer." When addressing real estate and financial matters in this book, I've taken every effort to ensure that I provide the most accurate information that allows you to grow your business and improve your life. However, there is no guarantee that you will get any results or earn any money using any of my ideas, tools, strategies or recommendations. This is not a "get rich scheme." Nothing in this book is a promise or guarantee of earnings. Your level of success in attaining similar results is dependent upon a number of factors including your skill, knowledge, ability, dedication, business savvy, network, and financial situation, to name a few. Because these factors differ according to individuals, I cannot, and do not guarantee your success, income level, or ability to earn revenue. You alone are responsible for your actions and results in life and business. Any forward-looking statements outlined in this book are simply my opinions and thus, are not guarantees or promises for actual performance. It should be clear to you that by law I make no guarantees that you will achieve any results from my ideas or models presented in this book, and I offer no professional legal, medical, psychological or financial advice.

WHAT'S IT WORTH TO YOU?
STEP 1: MEET WITH THE PROFESSIONAL

*"If you think hiring a pro is expensive,
wait until you hire an amature"*
– Red Adair

HOW GOOD IS YOUR PRODUCT? And by "product," I mean your house. When you post your home on the Multiple Listing Service (aka, the market) buyers will place a value on your house as it compares to the other houses on the market. "Product" is a fantastic word for a house listed on the market for sale. It conjures the idea that your home is a "good" to be bought and sold just like an item at the grocery store, except on a larger level…and with a lot more emotions. Actually, a ton more emotions (think of your average high school girl going through a breakup…on prom night…in a gym with no air conditioning…it's bad).

You might know you have a great home, but the beginning of marketing a house is to ensure others, namely any potential buyers, see that you have a great product too.

So, let's get to work on your "product." As a homeowner working to sell your house, there are only two aspects you really have control over; the **condition** and the **price**. That's it. You can't control the Real Estate Market anymore than I can. You can't control the economy. You can't control your neighbors who just put their house on the market for $50,000 more than it's worth or the other neighbor who underpriced at $50,000 less. All you have control over is the condition of your house and the price. The great thing is that if you take care of the condition, the price of your home usually takes care of itself.

So, let's focus on what we *can* control and get your product into killer shape!

STEP 1:
MEET WITH THE PROFESSIONAL

The first step is to meet with your real estate professional to discuss the current value of your house and to review the market conditions. There are a variety of ways to find the right professional for you, but I would suggest getting referrals from your friends and neighbors. From there, do research on the Real Estate Agent. Check their reviews, see their current listings, review their website, and make sure you get a positive feel from your research. After that, a simple phone call to ask any quick questions you have is a great idea before you set up an appointment. You want to ask the agent the following:

- What level of services do you provide?
- Why should I consider you over other agents?
- What do you charge?
- What experience do you have in my specific location/area?
- How often can I expect to hear from you?
- What is your marketing strategy?

You want a professional that has communication, service, and marketing as their top priorities. Selling a house without any feedback from your agent makes the home selling experience almost unbearable. Without ongoing communication, you have no idea what buyers are saying about your house, the active marketing efforts or what is going on in the market. This lack of communication strategy leaves homeowners in the dark and frustrated.

Service is an obvious criteria because you need to know what to expect from your professional. If you hire the cheapest Real Estate services you can find, don't be disappointed when they don't do any work to sell your house and your home sits on the market month after month. Know ahead of time what they offer so you don't get locked into a long term contract with a dud of an agent.

Marketing is one of the most important aspects your professional needs to cover. We joke in our industry that lazy agents do the "Triple P" **P**lace a sign in the yard, **P**ut it on the MLS (Multiple Listing Service) and **P**ray that it sells. They are all necessary (particularly prayer) but they are a start to marketing, not the only tools a professional should use.

After you have a few agents, or one you really like, schedule an appointment for them to meet with you at your house. You can expect the agent(s) to do a couple of things:

1. Take a tour of your home to assist with a market analysis and to start the discussion on possible repairs and updates needed.
2. Review the Comparative Market Analysis (CMA) to help determine your house's value.
3. Detail a marketing strategy.
4. Inform you about the status of the local real estate market.
5. Create a "Seller's Net Sheet" which is an estimated break down of your expenses at closing so you know what you will "net" on the sale of your house.

Best of luck with finding the right professional. Check out our YouTube Channel – The Holub Team, for some other great ideas of how to hire the right professional as well as other great videos expanding on the principles and steps in this book.

Now that you have a professional on your side, I want to get back to considering if updating your house is a solid return on your investment. Your professional will review a CMA (Comparative Market Analysis), which is a spreadsheet view of all the houses similar to yours. On this analysis will be properties like yours that are active on the market, pending with a contract, sold and even those that terminated from not finding a buyer. For you, at this time, the sold homes are the most important. This is because they will give the best indication of the market value of your house. Later in chapter 7, I will discuss extensively about pricing your home but for now, I want to evaluate and discover if it is worth updating or selling it in its current condition.

In the example CMA (Comparative Market Analysis) in Figure 1 below, a home owner's house is 2,750 sq. ft.(Square Feet), has 4 bedrooms, 2.5 bathrooms, does not have a pool, has a 2 car garage and was built in 2000. It has original laminate countertops in the kitchen, beige paint, along with builder grade countertops and tile in the bathrooms.

Address	SqFt	Bed	Bath	Gar.	Pool	List Price	List / SF.	Sold $	Sold $ /SF	List / Sell
Subject Property	2,750	4	2.5	2	N	?	?	?	?	?
243 Amber Ln.	2920	4	3.0	2	N	$325,000	$111.30	$317,000	$108.73	97.7%
392 Stout Heart Dr.	2,810	4	2.5	2	N	$275,000	$97.86	$275,000	$97.86	100%
14 Red Beard St.	2,740	4	2.5	2	N	$319,000	$116.42	$315,000	$114.96	98.7%
741 Pale Bale Ave.	2,450	4	2.5	2	N	$289,900	$118.32	$280,000	$114.28	96.6%

Figure 1

In the example CMA, there are 4 similar properties sold, ranging from 2,450 sq ft. to 2,920 sq ft. Here you can see the list price, sales price, and the percentage the homes sold for compared to the starting list price. We also see an average price per square foot rate

(List/SF), which is a simple guide to get a ballpark price evaluation for your home. The best way to determine the value of your home is to do a detailed market analysis that adds and removes value for updates, differences in lot size, interior square feet, and condition. I like to call this an "Appraiser CMA."

An "Appraiser CMA" helps to compare a honeycrisp apple to another honeycrisp apple of a different orchard. They are the same type of apple but if you look closely, they may have subtle differences. Most people will just use the price per square foot to compare to another house to see if it is a "good deal." While it is good to know, comparing two homes by their dollar per square foot is like comparing an orange to an apple. Both are fruit and sweet but, they are obviously very different. Your agent will most likely review a "simple CMA" with you but they can work up an "Appraiser CMA" after touring your house.

Okay, now that you have an understanding that we are speaking in "ballpark" numbers, let's head back to our example. The house at 392 Stout Heart Drive is in similar condition to the subject property, as well as having a similar size and layout. From the CMA we gather that an original home in the neighborhood will sell around $98/sq.ft. and an updated home will sell around $114/sq. ft. These number estimates would theoretically leave us with around $16/sqft. to improve the house which is around $44,000, without worrying about over-improving.

To bring the home up to the level of updates that 741 Pale Bale Ave & 14 Red Beard St, the homeowner will need to update the kitchen with new countertops, tile backsplash and updated flooring as well as the master bathroom with new countertops and floors. The entire house should be painted and if there's any money left over, update all hardware (door knobs, pulls, faucets and sometimes ceiling fans) and light fixtures to a consistent style. It can be very distracting to have shiny gold light fixtures with brushed nickel cabinet pulls.

If the homeowner can get the recommended updates completed for $20,000 to $24,000, then they should have an extra $20,000 of equity. Equity is the difference between the loan amount and the market value of a home. When you look at the numbers that way, of course it makes sense to update the house. After reaching that conclusion, a homeowner would then need to discuss if the necessary funds are available and if the family is willing to live in a construction zone for a few months.

On the other hand, say the house has been updated throughout the time it has been lived in, but not quite as nice as the extensive remodel in the previous example. The goal then would be to maximize the value of the sale price with minimal renovations because it does not have as much distance to get to the top end of the market. Over-improving a house is all too common, unfortunately. Fresh paint on the wall, a few updated light fixtures and upgraded hardware (handles & knobs) could provide a great return at minimal cost and help sell the house more quickly and without breaking the bank.

Most of the homeowners I work with can better relate to the later example. Usually, they have been diligent with repairs and even a few updates from time to time. However, they just need a little more work and attention to help their house sell quickly for the max return. I wouldn't suggest doing any updates or repairs to your house until you meet with your real estate professional to discuss whether it will provide either a return on investment in price or a shorter time on the market (more on that later).

With all of that said, if it makes sense to update your house, meeting with a designer would be the next step. A designer will help to determine what colors and updates will work within the budget. Many designers can be very affordable and can provide just the right amount of guidance you need to make the right design choices. So, I ask again, what's it worth to you?

ACTION PLAN:

- Meet with a real estate professional to discuss the current value of your house and its potential value after updating.

- If updating is a good fit, then begin working with a professional designer and contractor to determine the best updates to add, projected costs and timeframe.

PREPARE YOUR HOUSE & PLAN TO WIN
STEP 2: DE-CLUTTER & DE-PERSONALIZE

"The meeting of preparation with opportunity generates the offspring we call luck."
– Tony Robbins

THE WAY YOU LIVE IN A HOME, and the way you sell a home are two completely different things. I like to help our homeowners begin detaching from their home by calling it a "house" rather than a "home." While this may seem like a small semantic difference, it evokes a completely different set of emotions. You and your spouse excitedly bring your first child "home" from the hospital. The living room in your "home" is where you spend time opening up Christmas and birthday gifts. In the backyard of your "home," your kiddos played on the swing set you painstakingly assembled. Simply put, a "home" is where you create and share wonderful memories. "Home" recalls how you scrimped and saved just enough to get a down payment together. "Home" is a charged word that conjures emotions and for most of us, wonderful memories.

A house is just a place to store your items and to sleep at night. A house is something you drive by and think, "that house has nice shutters." It feels less personal, like an object that you just happen to own…or not. A house on the market is a "product" that is being sold. A house is a product for which buyers evaluate and negotiate a price, depending on how it compares to the other houses on the market. It is not personal to the buyers of your house; they are just looking for a great deal. From now on, I will refer to your property as a "house" and to your buyers new house (your old one) as a "home."

It is all a matter of perspective. Now that you no longer see your house as your home, but as a "product" to market and sell, it is time to move on. I know, that was quick. I have magic abilities. Now for my next trick, getting you to finally clear out that guest bedroom. The next step will be to start preparing the best product possible.

STEP #2:
DE-CLUTTER & DE-PERSONALIZE YOUR HOUSE

Okay, now I have to be the bad guy. As discussed in the last chapter, it is important to remember what these steps are worth to you. For the time being, you will need to remove your personal items from the decor of the house. These are the items that make it a home for you and your family. For example, but not limited too; your family pictures, political paraphernalia, pet items, and any unique art or distracting furniture. As tough as this process can be, it is important to remove any family pictures from the walls. This step is paramount. A potential buyer will have a hard enough time as it is picturing their items and their lives within the walls of your house. This becomes much, much harder when your beautiful family is all over the walls in framed images.

Remember, we want the buyers to walk in and feel like they have come home, and not like they are just intruding into your home and space. We want potential buyers to envision their furniture, their family, and their future in the house. Following this step thoroughly, helps to eliminate the distractions of your lovely family and decor, allowing buyers to experience what it would be like to call your house their home. We want them to spend 20 minutes imagining how their furniture will fit in the living area for optimal entertaining experiences, what decorations they will add and how the floor plan will work with parties and large family gatherings.

Therefore, it's time to put on your "buyer glasses," and take a step back and see your house the way a potential buyer might see it. Do not be blinded by how you have seen your house for the years you have lived there. When you see something every day it tends to lose its impact and fades into the background. There are things in your house that you have settled with that don't even occur to you as needing attention anymore. For example, that scuff on the hallway wall that has been there for longer than you would care to admit, overtime it just becomes part of the wall to you. However, to a potential buyer, that scuff is HUGE and therefore the entire hallway needs repainting.

Take a fresh look through the eyes of a buyer to see what they see when visiting your house. A good idea would be to take a roll of painters tape and do a "blue tape walk-through." Really look high and low, and note all the items that need attention to help your house get into prime condition. Only when you, the current homeowner and seller, are honest with the condition of your house will you understand what really needs to be addressed. The things that stand out to you, most certainly will stand out to buyers.

After storing away your photos and doing a walkthrough of your house, it is time to work on styling. It is always good to make sure that your home decorations are neutral and not too distracting. While renaissance nude paintings may be beautiful, it could deter your future buyer from making an offer. I once had a client that had a wonderful collection of Native American art, but I was worried it would deter future buyers from seeing the beauty of the house. I had our stager come in to help remove many of the items but leave a few of the more important items from the collection on display. This allowed for a few of the more stellar pieces to be showcased, in particular, ones that were important to the homeowner. Overall, this "less is more mentality," left us with a uniquely decorated house while not being overbearing to potential buyers. The home sold within a couple of weeks even with a good amount of competition in the neighborhood.

As I have already mentioned, you will need to remove your family pictures from the walls and shelves. Then comes the question, of what do you put in their place? Some simple art or landscape pictures can really jazz up a room without taking over, and you can usually find some inexpensive prints if you look hard enough. Currently, there is a decor trend of having different motivational phrases hung on the wall as art, this is a great option as well.

Next up, smells. Our sense of smell is tied to our memory. Pleasant smells, lead to pleasant memories. Poor smells lead to poor memories (deep stuff, I know). It is important to be aware how your house smells in order for it not to be a negative distraction to potential buyers. You want buyers to remember how great your house is and it's beauty, and not how poorly it smelled. Strong ethnic food smells, pet odor, cat pee, incense, smoke and many others have deterred many of my clients from purchasing otherwise great homes. I had a buyer who found the perfect home, at the perfect price, and in the perfect location who chose to pass on the house. The problem, you guessed it, cats. There was an overwhelming smell of cat pee, making this perfect home choice, not so puurrrfect. Get a smell test. Ask your most brutally honest friends and neighbors to give you their opinion of what they think of the smell in your house.

Proctor & Gamble did extensive research before they released Febreze to the national market. They focused on homeowners that had "over the top" smelly homes. This included homes with multiple pets (at the point of being a hoarder house) to see if their product would really work. Time and time again, the homeowners were unable to notice how terrible their homes really were as they just got "used to" the smell. The product was almost scrapped because the researchers couldn't figure out how to get the homeowners that truly needed the product to recognize that they had a smelly problem. It obviously went on to be a huge success, but it goes to show how we desensitized we get to our own "house smell." (Febreze Case Study[2])

Do whatever you can to get your home to a refreshing but neutral scent. Something like a light clean linen scent usually goes well with many buyers. With that all said, don't just cover up a bad smell, if an area needs a deep cleaning, for example carpets and draperies, then do so. Natural oils are becoming more and more popular. Getting a diffuser with a few oils such as lavender, peppermint, and cinnamon and see which one you like the most. These oils are wonderful and can even provide health benefits. Check online for great essential oil blends for your diffuser to find the right smell for your house.

A house is made of many walls. Painting or at least paint touch ups, are vital. If a homeowner hasn't placed a fresh coat of paint on the walls in a while or if they have made some strong color choices in the past, then I always suggest painting. Painting a neutral color that is currently popular is almost always a winning idea and something to run by the designer. I suggest adding your "fun" colors through art, throw pillows and other items rather than a bold color on the wall. You'd be surprised how much a new coat of paint really makes a home feel fresh and inviting to a buyer. It also is a great return on investment as a $50 paint can may add up to $1,000 once it's on the wall.

One of my clients had a beautiful house for sale. It was older and wasn't the most up-to-date house, but it had a great layout and a great charm to it. I didn't even suggest painting as I thought their banana yellow walls actually worked with the house, but they decided to paint the entire interior and exterior before hitting the market. When I first walked in, I knew something was different but couldn't quite put my finger on it. The house felt more calming and open. It wasn't until the homeowner told me they painted the walls neutral grey with a tint of blue that I took notice. It looked amazing! I can hardly express what a difference it made on the house other than that buyers felt it too. We had three offers within five days after a list price at the higher end for the neighborhood.

At the back of this book on page 145 is a room by room checklist for getting your house ready for the stager. Make sure to review this resource to get a detailed idea of specific tasks and other items to help with a game plan for your perfectly staged house.

ACTION PLAN

- Your home will be a product on the open market, it's time to begin detaching and taking an honest look at the condition of your house.

- De-personalize your house: remove family pictures, unique art and decorations, refrigerator art, political items and so forth.

- De-clutter your house: put away extra furniture, overcrowded books from bookshelves, toys, clutter, bills and so forth.

HOMEWORK
STEP 3: DO NECESSARY REPAIRS & UPDATES

"In the middle of every diffviculty lies opportunity"
– Albert Einstein

SHOULD I UPDATE MY KITCHEN or just sell it "as is"? Should I put on a new roof? Does this exterior paint color make my house look fat? I get these and other similar property questions all the time and my answer is almost always, "depends." Not because I support adult diapers, but because there are many factors that contribute to the right answer. A few of the variables are:

- What is the current condition of the house?

- What is the quality level and age of the current upgrades?

- Is the style & design consistent throughout?

- What is the current value of the home vs. the potential return on investment from potential upgrades?

- What are the top-end sale prices of homes in your neighborhood?

- What are the current market trends?

- What kind of cash is available for repairs/updates?

- and so on...

This chapter we will look at a few ideas to help you think about what you may need to work on to maximize the value in your house. I beg, often times on my hands and knees, for clients to not do any repairs or updates unless they run it by myself or their real estate professional. If they are at all worried about resale, and they should be worried, then they need to know they are making the right updates or to understand that their efforts won't bring them much increased value when they decide to sell. There are many homes that I tour where the owner tells me they just "updated" it for sale. This always scares the stuffing out of me, mostly because homeowners almost always spend money on items that won't bring the best return on investment or they put in dated "updates."

For example, one homeowner's house I walked into had contractors in the house and they were just finishing up the remodel, but my heart sank when I saw four different tile flooring styles, dated appliances, and some shoddy work. The kitchen had a new granite countertop but all the appliances were original and that included a tiny oven and the original coiled electric stove. The master bathroom had some updates, but it still clung to the 70's with all it's might.

Now, there is nothing wrong with any of those things. You can be perfectly happy in a house that is original; Love makes a house a home. But in regards to resale, it would almost have been better for the homeowner's return on investment to leave the house "as is" rather than updating it.

Buyers will pay a premium to have a "move-in ready" home. Buyers can see where they will put their furniture and how they will decorate, rather than focusing on what they will need to do just to have it livable to their standards and preferences. If they walk around your house and start subtracting money from the list price in their head, then it usually don't result in an solid offer.

With the popularity of HGTV, and sites like Pinterest and Houzz, buyers expect to walk into beautifully remodeled homes with all the latest updates and features for a minimal budget. It is frustrating for many homeowners who have beautiful, well-cared-for homes but may not have the latest color or trendy backsplash. When meeting with new clients, If the homeowner has a full remodeling budget and some room with the upper-end of the market, then we talk about what updates would bring the return they are looking for.

Take a look at Figure 2 on the following page to see a sample of data from the Cost vs. Value Report 2018[1] that compares popular remodeling projects with their resale value.

Cost vs. Value for Popular Remodeling Projects

Remodeling Project	NARI Estimated Cost	Realtors Estimate Cost Recovery	Percent of Return
Complete Kitchen Remodel	$65,000	$40,000	62%
Kitchen Upgrade	$35,000	$20,000	57%
Master Bathroom Renovation	$30,000	$15,000	50%
New Wood Flooring	$5,500	$5,000	91%
Add a Bathroom	$59,000	$30,000	50%
Hardwood Floor Refinish	$3,000	$3,000	100%
New Master Suite	$125,000	$65,000	52%
HVAC Replacement	$7,500	$5,000	67%
Closet Renovation	$37,500	$2,000	53%
Insulation Upgrade	$2,100	$1,600	76%

Figure 2

It may surprise you to know that a majority of renovation projects do not provide a great return on investment. Just because you extended out the master bathroom and put in a shower the size of a football field with five super sprayer shower heads that could clean a mastodon, doesn't mean you will get to add every dollar you spent on top of the market value of your house. It typically means you should get a portion of it back, but not always.

Do keep in mind that many of these numbers are national averages and could be high or low for your area. Also, I do believe that if you spent $10k on improvements, it is possible to get $20k in return or more, otherwise investors would always lose money when they flip a house.

However, most homeowners don't have a bunch of cash to drop on remodeling, most have a small amount of money for repairs and a few minor updates. If you are "asking for a friend," what updates to do on a budget? Then you're in luck! Here are some lower cost items that can have an enormous return.

UPDATES ON A BUDGET

Paint can be your best friend. As I mentioned before, A $50 gallon of paint on the wall can mean as much as an additional $1,000 in resale value. Talk about a good return! If you have had any ceiling repairs, cracks in the wall, or previous remodeling throughout the years, chances are your ceiling and wall texture may be a little like patchwork in some places. It may be a good idea to have a professional scrape the texture or feather in some more texture so that is looks like seamless work. It will provide a consistent, fresh new look and feel less like they are walking into a major project. A designer can help with the wall colors that are neutral and trendy as well as what works with your current home decor.

If your budget doesn't allow for a professional painter, then make sure that you don't sacrifice quality. Paint the ceiling, paint the trim, paint the walls, touch up or redo texture and be sure to caulk where it's needed. I toured a home for sale and you could clearly tell the homeowners had painted the walls themselves. How could I tell you ask? Throughout the house the tapelines were spotty, the previous wall color was showing through in some places, the master bedroom walls were an excrement brown color and there wasn't a thread of interior design. So if you paint, make sure you do a top notch job or just send to a professional.

New hardware throughout the house can quickly bring a dated house to the 21st century. Hardware refers to the door knobs, handles, cabinet pulls, and faucets. I tend to even lump in ceiling fans and light fixtures too, because they tend to be the same color from when the house was originally built. For example, replacing all the hardware with the original gold finish to an oiled bronze hardware provides a cohesive feel throughout the house. It could cost you a couple hundred bucks and half a Saturday, but this simple update could also help your house to sell faster and for a couple grand more.

Another quick update that can have a dramatic impact is to change out the kitchen backsplash. Let's say you have a natural stone countertop but you still have the builder grade tile backsplash from the early 2000's. It doesn't look bad, but it is not the current, most popular finish. Thus, It would be very cost effective to have a contractor demo and retile a backsplash with more modern colors and materials. Of course, I highly recommend running this by the designer or stager helping you.

The best location in the house to spend your update dollars is in the kitchen, master suite, and flooring throughout the house. The kitchen is number one on the list of priorities. Most people spend a majority of their time while home in the kitchen; cooking, eating, doing homework, or entertaining. It's the central hub of the house and is seen by all guests. There is a reason it is called the "Heart of the Home." Even if my clients eat out every night of the week, they still always want an updated and current kitchen. Thus, it is important to give the area a current update if needed. If your budget allows for renovations beyond the kitchen, I recommend the master suit and bathroom as well as flooring throughout.

Lighting is another great way to update a house. Ample natural light with indoor/outdoor living space is crazy desirable for today's home buyers. As expected, it is pretty expensive to put in floor to ceiling windows, but opening the blinds and removing any solar screens or tinted window film will maximize the light coming into the home. Recessed lights are great but can be expensive as well, and if you are scared of working with that black magic like I am, electrical repairs I mean, don't mess with it.

Undermount cabinet lighting can be amazing. If you don't have wiring for lights under the upper cabinets in your kitchen or wherever else you have built-in shelving, then check out some of the LED battery powered products available. They often look just as good as the wired light installations. More light is great, just don't go overboard. Red and green tinted lights are probably not the best idea, even at Christmas.

Refinishing hardwood floors can be a great "Do It Yourself" project and according to the Cost vs. Value Report of 2018[1], it often provides 100% return on your investment. Other flooring ideas on a budget would include having the carpets cleaned or replaced. If you have four different tile floorings throughout your first floor, and they all connect at some point, it needs to be changed so that a cohesive feel can be achieved.

Finally, refinishing or painting the front door is a great idea and should be near the top of your "To Do" list. Your front door is a little preview to buyers as to what to expect when entering your house. It is the first thing buyers, and the potential new home owners' guests will notice. A freshly refinished or painted door can say a lot about what lies beyond it.

REPAIRS

Repairs, just like updates, are very specific to your part of the country, so just adapt some of these items to your area. It is important to understand that most repairs will not add any value to your sales price. However, not doing your do diligence in these matters, will lend to a price drop if uncompleted home maintenance is too obvious or burdensome to potential buyers. Again, buyers want a "move-in ready" home, and not a "honey-do list" from day one.

A basic rule of thumb is, if it is a distraction, it is best to eliminate it. If something needs to be repaired for max resale value, or if the system in question in its current state, will cause the majority of buyers to be turned away, then you are better off completing the repair yourself. If not, your sales price can easily be affected.

For example, multiple diagonal cracks above the door frames throughout a house is a tell-tale sign of foundation issues. If you desire your house to be sold at top-dollar, it needs to have the foundation and then the sheetrock repaired. Also, any water stains on the ceiling, whether active or dry for many years, tells the buyer that there is a leak and it could lead to more issues that are beyond just a quick fix. In a buyer's mind, the leak has been going on for years and has created mold in the subfloor, rotted out joist, attracted carpenter ants and will cause the house to implode at any moment (this is the most likely scenario, naturally). Correctly addressing the problem and disclosing it is the best course of action.

Roof, HVAC, electrical & water heaters are all major components to your house. Deciding if something should be replaced can be an expensive proposition, and a struggle for many homeowners. If these integral systems to your home are approaching the end of their normal life but still working as intended, I would normally advise not to replace them. For one reason, you never know what is going to be a concern for the buyer. What if you install a new AC system to replace a 20 year old air condition and spend $6,500 when the buyer would have bought the house at the same price and would have been happy to split the replacement cost and be provided with a home warranty?

Or you replace a perfectly working 30-year composite shingle roof that only has five years of life left because you are worried the buyer will be too skittish to move forward for a similar outcome.

Another reason to not make too many repairs to working components in your house is that it usually doesn't add much value to the sale of your house. A new hot water heater is great, but it won't add to a higher sales price. Many times, a buyer purchases a home because the cosmetic updates draw them in, and any items noted on the inspection report in need of repair can usually be addressed for less. As long as the repair list is not too long, and you are willing to work with them, MOST buyers are happy to move forward. Their goal after all, is to purchase a great house.

Small repairs such as caulking, replacing rotting siding, regrouting tile, and so on should be done as much as possible to provide the "move-in ready" feel. Be careful! If you are doing the work yourself, make sure the work doesn't scream "do-it-yourself" repair. Many times a weekend warrior's work can be worse than if it was left alone. Save any receipts of work completed, done by you or a professional, to share with your future buyer.

Depending upon the price point of your house, it may not be prudent to replace the single paned windows with energy efficient ones. I know it says otherwise in the Housing Preferences of the Boomer Generation study by the National Association of Builders, but in my experience, I don't see a great return on investment for sellers that have full window replacements. I normally suggest not replacing them if interior cosmetics are not fully updated. Although, if there are other upgrades, and there is money in the budget, replacing just a few windows around the house, particularly if you remodeled certain areas like the kitchen, master suite and living areas, can be a great idea. Only replacing a few of the windows still provides a clean, energy efficient feel without breaking the bank.

If you are not able to complete all needed repairs and you are consistently getting feedback that buyers are concerned with the carpet, wall colors or whatever the complaints of the day, then it may be a good idea to provide a credit to them upfront, so they can replace the item of concern. I don't often recommend this, as it would be better to paint or install the carpet yourself, most buyers have no imagination and need to see it already taken care of. However, in some cases, taking care of the repairs yourself may not be financially possible. If a credit is the route you take, make sure you tape a sign over the area of concern informing the buyer of the concession along with having your agent make a note in the MLS listing. All things are negotiable so make sure the item is clearly written in your contract when finalizing your sale.

Okay, I know that's a lot of great info but I want to make sure you get a great bang for your buck. What I want to make clear from this chapter is :

1. You can spend money in the wrong places and not get a return on investment.
2. Meet with the professionals to make sure you are maximizing your repair dollars.
3. Repairs and updates don't have to break the bank and many small items can have a tremendous impact.

It may cost some money to work with a designer or stager, a real estate professional, and contractor; but in the end, you should see a better return than if you went all Rambo on your house in your preparations for sale.

ACTION PLAN:

- Meet with the right professionals before doing any updates: designer/stager, real estate professional & contractor(s).

- Determine how much money and time you have to invest in updating your house.

- Create a game plan to hit your targeted sales price by the number of updates you undertake.

PRETTY HOUSES SELL
STEP 4: STAGE THE HOUSE TO GET IT IN THE BEST SHAPE

"You never get a second chance
to make a first impression"
– Will Rogers

STAGING IS QUITE POSSIBLY one of the best returns on investments you can do for your home. This is the process of arranging furniture and decorations in the most attractive way possible; think of a home builder's model home as a great example because they always feel inviting, modern and it just makes you want to buy the house. The process of staging can be as involved as renting furniture, artwork and doing a variety of updates, or simply just working with the furniture and decorations you already have in your home.

Staging your house can be likened to getting ready for your first date. You put on your best outfit, do a smell test to make sure your clothes are clean and you make sure to put on a copious amount of deodorant (pit check anyone?). When on your date, you put your best foot forward and are conscious to "hide your crazy." You want your house to make a similar first impression. This impression happens the minute the buyers drive up to the front of the house. Following the recommendations of a good stager, you will have your home decorated with only the nicest furniture & decorations you have, clutter & personal items removed, the best air fresheners, and you will have made sure that any "crazy" you have is hidden (yes, that means your extensive Russian nesting doll collection).

The great news is that for a few hours of your time and for a minimal amount of money you can usually add some extra cash at closing, often thousands. According to the National Association of Realtors® and the *2017 Profile of Home Buyers*[6], 31% of buyers' agents believe that staging a home increases the dollar value offered between one and five percent compared to other similar homes on the market that are not staged. Think it's worth your time? I think so, and that is why I always recommend meeting with a staging professional and often pay for a 3-hour professional consultation. It can be difficult to shell out a couple hundred bucks on a stager, but if you end up selling for a few grand more, and have less time on the market, which equals fewer holding costs, then your return on investment is out of the park!

A stager (that's a funny term, I'm glad we are called Reatlors® and not "housers," that would just be strange...but I digress) is a home design professional that specializes in preparing your house for sale. They can either work with the items you own to maximize the beauty of your house or they may rent furniture for you if it's empty (or if you just have a terrible sense of style. Hey, it happens).

STEP #4:
STAGE THE HOUSE TO GET IT IN ITS BEST SHAPE

I highly recommend setting up a meeting with a staging professional. If you don't have furniture in your house, it may be the best thing for you to do. A staged home sells faster than a vacant or "normal" lived-in-home. This is because many buyers "see" and "feel" how a "house" can become "home." And mostly, because most people don't have any imagination of what a room can look like unless you show them. Back in the day, the prevalent thinking was that a vacant home sells better than a lived in home. In some cases that is true, but for the most part, having furniture in the house with other tasteful decorations is the best way to sell a house.

While a detailed discussion of housing design trends is beyond the scope of this book, I will discuss some overarching themes that are timeless with home staging. Your professional stager will fill in the gaps and keep you up to date on the latest trends.

CURB APPEAL

Let's start from the outside in, just the way your buyer will experience the house. Curb appeal is often overlooked when preparing a home for sale. There is often so much to do on the interior that the outdoors is frequently neglected. As modern home builders have focused more attention on developing beautiful exterior elevations with a mixture of textures, materials, and colors, it is less likely for you to need much work if your home was built more recently. Many of the homes built in the 60's-80's often have a unique style that needs a little more work creating an inviting exterior.

Some homes may need to have their pink tinted brick painted (guilty). Or to have the weird fenced in patio in your front yard removed (guilty again). Or remove the large bird fountain with the giant stone hand opening up to the sky like it's ready to grab the next bird that lands on it, but you haven't removed it because it was given to you by your previous real estate agent when you closed on your house (not guilty, you laugh but the struggle is real). I suggest removing these types of items or any extremely dated designs to not be a deterrent to potential buyers from seeing a great home, inside and out.

If your house has a traditional style, kick it up a notch but don't go too far outside its original design. If you have a mid-century modern home, stay true to the build when you modernize it. If you have a craftsman style home built in the early 20th century, rock that like a flapper doing the Charleston. When homeowner's updates and design don't flow with the construction of the house, buyers tend to feel the disconnect. I once toured a traditional ranch floor plan that was traditional on the exterior, but Greek Parthenon on the inside. It was nice, but it felt off with the design, and many buyers agreed as it was on the market for a long while. This does not preclude you from making a ranch home a French country dream house or an eco-friendly contemporary masterpiece. I'm just saying, it all needs to flow from exterior to interior. To go outside the original build and style of a home dramatically usually takes a professional's touch.

I have discussed many general repairs you should complete to maximize your return with little costs, but now I'll review some of the room specific items. I may sound like a broken record, but you can almost never go wrong with some fresh exterior paint (unless you pick a hideous color). The next update that is almost a sure-fire improvement is to refinish or install a new front door. It serves as an accent piece to your house and a solid, beautiful door not only looks good, but it feels good as the buyer opens it to the wonders inside. I'm a sucker for solid wood doors with a small amount of glass at the top or some side lights to allow extra natural light into your entry. Too much glass and buyers get worried about safety and privacy, not enough makes the first impression of your house feel like a buyer has walked into a dungeon.

Another tip on the choice of front doors is to make sure it flows with the rest of the house. Don't buy the 'ye olde medieval wood front door' with the wrought iron frame hardware and the working speakeasy trap door if you have sleek and modern decor inside. It just won't flow. How a house flows is very important and something that I'll come back to often. As mentioned in chapter 3, you want your front door to be a little "sneak peek" of the amazing design they will find inside. A new set of door hardware, a new front door mat and a seasonal wreath always help to achieve this as well.

If you have a front yard, put down fresh mulch in your flower beds and plant some flowers to add color during the warmer months. I always recommend black mulch or natural color mulch but if you must, you can use red mulch, but only if you have a complimentary colored exterior. It's best to stay safe with the black or natural mulch. This creates the fresh feeling we want the buyers to have. Fresh landscaping, fresh exterior paint, fresh front door (too much fresh?) provides the buyer with a splendid feeling like they are going to walk into something wonderful.

If your shrubs and bushes have been growing for 20+ years, it may be a good idea to save up some money to remove the old shrubs and plant some fresh landscaping (if he says "fresh" one more time...). Many homeowners have had their front bushes growing for decades. They don't realize how much the oversized shrubs detract from the beauty of the house. Trim those trees, let more light in the yard, and allow the buyers to see the home.

This too may go without saying, but I'm gonna say it...make sure your lawn is well manicured. I can't tell you how many times I have driven up to a house to tour it with a buyer, and the yard hasn't been cut in weeks, the grass is a pale yellow, there are copious amounts of weeds in the flowerbeds, and all the annuals have died but are still lingering in the beds. This lack of attention is definitely a turn off to any potential buyer. Keep your lawn green, mow it weekly, pull those weeds, and if your annuals die, remove them. It may be worth the cost to hire a professional for a few weeks to get the lawn in top shape than to try to do it yourself.

If you don't have a yard, look at what a buyer sees when they are first entering your condo, townhouse or apartment. Think about what you can do to add a little "pop" to stand out. What flowering plants or bushes would work for your front porch or entryway? See what control the homeowners association will give you to make changes to your front exterior to make it more inviting. Some condo and apartment entryways are dimly light and are smelly, so see what additional light can be added, and if power washing is an option.

Make sure all exterior lights are working, dust and cobwebs are removed, the mailbox is in good condition, and to remove any kid toys from the front yard (and driveway, and backyard and trees…I have kids, I know your struggle).

Finally, make sure that you really play up any positive aspects the front exterior may have. If you have a front porch, put in a swing with some inviting pillows and some potted plants. If you have a great front yard with a huge shade tree, put in two adirondack chairs under it with some colorful exterior pillows to give the buyers a sense of community in the neighborhood, along with conveying the idea that they can relax even in the front yard. Do something different that helps your home to stand out, as well as for buyers to experience snapshots of the life they can live if they purchase your house.

STAGING THE LIVING AREAS

On to the interior of the home! In its simplest form, staging a home consists of:

1. Decluttering.
2. De-Personalizing.
3. Delighting the buyers.

You will see me hit back on these three points multiple times so it's a good idea to get them memorized. There is an amazing detailed checklist on page 145 in the book so be sure to check off those important items.

Declutter — This means to remove your junk and clutter, which you already did right after you read chapter 2, right? (riiiiight…I'll wait…). People ask me if it's okay to have their treasure (aka junk) stored in the garage, and it absolutely is! Buyers would rather see it out of the house and boxed up than overcrowding their tour. Plus, potential buyers will totally understand, after all, you are moving.

De-Personalize — You have a very specific set of likes and dislikes regarding your home's design, we need to remove those touches and create a product that buyers believe THEY can personalize. It is important to give the feel of a blank canvas of a home, but finding balance to help give ideas of what a space can be. Don't be offended when the stager asks you to hide your extensive beanie baby collection or other unique items. The stager knows what needs to be presented and what needs to be tucked away inside your house. It is your job to trust them. With these tasks, and any other suggestions of your stager, following them is your choice. Staging your house in the right way and following a professional's advice for an increased return...or not, is your call. Either way, you have a game plan and your results will be dependant upon how well you execute it.

Delight the Buyer — Staging doesn't have to mean a vast wasteland of soulless neutral decor. Staging should provide "wow" moments of design and features that will stand out in your buyer's mind. Put yourself in your buyer's shoes, after seeing about 6 houses in a row, they all start to run together. The goal is to have your house stand out from the "sameness" that is your competition, and any other home the potential buyers have seen.

Alright, so put your "buyer glasses" back on as we discuss staging the living areas of your house. More often than not, my buyers will walk into the entry of a house, then through the living room to spend time in the kitchen. If the kitchen doesn't suit their fancy, then the house is usually taken off the list. It is wise to focus on the areas a buyer will pass through to get to the kitchen. So, we will spend a good portion of our staging discussion on the most important zones.

Starting with the front entryway, it should be inviting but simple. The 4'x6' family portrait with everyone looking slightly to the left makes buyers feel like they are intruding in a strangers home (or even worse...that they are being watched). As we talked about before, the portrait needs to come down. Replace it with a neutral painting which can be found near any starving artist, or home decor store.

It's a great idea to have a flyer on your property in the front entryway for the buyers to refer to as they walk around the house. Your real estate professional will more than likely already have such a flyer on hand. Buyers will use this to remember your home later. "Marge, was that home 17 or 39? I can't remember."

Buyers usually move quickly to the living areas to see if they like the layout of the living room and kitchen. It's helpful to have as much natural light as possible so leave the blinds open, take off the exterior window covers and leave on a few well-placed lamps. If you do open up the blinds, just make sure buyers are looking at something nice (and not the compost pile). Ample natural light creates a great recipe for an inviting and warm living room.

Regarding living room furniture, it is okay to have your staging professional move pieces around, even if it doesn't make for the best TV watching experience. By having less furniture stationed around the fireplace or facing pieces more toward the kitchen, the room exudes a better feel for entertaining. This rearrangement often looks better than making the TV the strongest focal point. If buyers really like the layout, they will discuss where they will put their TV and how their furniture will fit in the space.

Your staging professional can assist with making sure you have a neutral color scheme, along with a few brighter items that pop out. A few new throw pillows, a cozy blanket draped across the couch, an interesting book open on the coffee table, and some decorative candles are all simple things that increase the appeal to a buyer, but carry minimal cost. Most of the time you already have all the items on hand and just need some assistance creating the "Model Home" vibe.

Be sure to remove any pet beds or cat towers as they will turn off any buyer that doesn't want a house that had pets. If they couldn't smell the pets when they came in, that's a great thing. Don't ruin it. If you have kids, remove the toys to their bedrooms or their playroom. Where ever they are, be sure that they are stored in an organized fashion. If you have to leave them in the living room, hide them in decorative storage containers or put them away in cabinets.

On to the kitchen! The kitchen is often the most important room to a buyer. Your buyer is first going to look at the layout, size and how the kitchen flows to the dining and living rooms. If it's not what they are looking for, it doesn't matter how nice the rest of the rooms are, they won't buy your house. So, don't be disheartened, it's not you...it's them. You most likely won't be able to cost effectively rework the layout of your kitchen, but you can help maximize the space to help find the right buyer—one that will fall in love with all your "cooking" assets.

One way to do that is to create emotional connection points (stager speak). Emotional connection points are feelings your visitors get when they tour your house, see how you live, and desire what you have (i.e. your house). Buyers are not just buying four walls and a yard. They are buying what a house can bring them; security, status, family memories, a trendy lifestyle, and so much more. If you can hit those desires then you can help your house to connect on a deeper level with your buyer.

It can be compared with buying an Apple product. Not only does it get the job of calling, emailing, texting and surfing the web done, but many users feel connected with the company's "against the grain" thinking. And while there may be a better product out there, the purchase of said product says more about the consumer and what it represents to them, that they just continue to buy it.

So, how does this relate to selling a house?

It is more difficult but still very possible. Back in the kitchen, showing the breakfast bar with stools and place settings displays a great place for eating and visiting while you cook. A bottle of wine and some wine glasses to give the feeling of a great entertaining space. Adding a pot, a few dry ingredients on the counter and a cookbook provides the visual of a great place to cook and evokes the feeling of home. Placing some homework with a book and a lamp on the desk in the kitchen recalls the feeling of the family all working in the same space together.

Make sure that you match the staging with your style of house. If your house is ultra sleek and modern, your buyer doesn't want to see homework and cooking. It may be geared more toward a buyer that likes to entertain but doesn't cook often, so make it a posh entertaining kitchen. That's right, I said posh...well, typed it, actually.

Back to my mantra: Declutter, Depersonalize and Delight!

Declutter — Make sure that you remove just about everything off your counters. You want to show them off and not let the counter space feel cluttered. Clean out your refrigerator and pantry. Buyers will open all doors. They want to to see if you are actually living in the house or not. Inquisitive creatures buyers are, are they not? Make sure the cabinets inside and outside are clean, items organized and all dishes in the sink and counter are removed and put away.

Depersonalize — Remove your kids drawings from the refrigerator, hide the bills from the counter, and put away any leftover food.

Delight the Buyer — Turn on undermount or up-lighting. Indirect lights have an inviting feel and are strongly recommended. Review the great updates in chapter three to provide an awesome return on your investment. You can also check out my site, TheRealEstateGamePlan.com to sign up for *"The Best Inexpensive Updates & Repairs to Do Prior to Selling Your Home."*

With appliances I always suggest staying with the level of upgrades that you have currently for your house. If your house has new countertops, backsplash, and flooring, but you still have the 30 year old appliances, then just know that they are a huge distraction to future buyers. Not replacing them with everything else creates an instant suspicion as to why you didn't fully upgrade the kitchen. They will also wonder what else you cheaped out on.

Fresh flowers are always a hit. If the market tends be slower, and the days on the market are long, just pace yourself on your flower budget and please be sure to replace them from time to time. Dead flowers don't give off a great "buy me now" vibe. Do make sure you show off any great views the house has, such as the relaxing pool, outdoor entertaining, or the 20 acres of green pastures. Flex indoor/outdoor living space is very popular and can help sell your house instantly.

Spend most of your time staging the kitchen and your living room as that is where most buyers decide if they will purchase or pass on your house. Little changes can go a long way. Discuss with your professionals what specifically you should do to maximize your space.

STAGING THE MASTER

My wife's aunt's father (huh?) received his masters degree while his wife earned her PhD in education. He used to joke, that he had no issues with calling his wife "doctor," as long as she addressed him as "master." I laughed for a solid ten minutes the first time I heard that. For some reason my wife doesn't care for calling me bachelor Paul.

Speaking of "master," let's talk about the master bedroom. Next to the kitchen and living room, this is the third most important area in your house. Be sure to declutter and keep it simple with a bed, night stands and maybe a few other pieces of furniture if space allows. Leave everything off the night stands except for a lamp and maybe a few other well placed decorations. Stagers call it the "rule of three" when you have three different sized decorations: small, medium and large. A large item on a nightstand is usually a lamp, then something medium sized such as a plant, candle or some art, paired along with an item that is smaller like a book or jewelry box. The variance in height and the minimal amount of objects, creates a visually pleasing flow, and is easy to do. Speaking of minimal and pleasing, don't leave the elliptical out that has become a clothes rack or the pile of bills that seem to have permanently found a place in the corner of the room for buyers to see.

Again, lighting is important. Lamps are fantastic and provide a great ambiance. Overhead lights from ceiling fans, not so great. Especially if only one of the four bulbs are working. If your master suite has french doors or windows leading to a great backyard or balcony, make sure to open the shades and show off the view, otherwise, make sure the master the focus.

Depersonalizing your bedroom doesn't just mean hiding of your favorite pillow (or teddy bear), just like the rest of the house, it also means removing oversized furniture. All too often when I am touring homes, we will walk into a bedroom that is 14x13 with 8 ft ceilings with a massive four-post bed with an oversized dresser and two ginormous night stands. All of this bulky furniture makes the room feel claustrophobic, tight, and worst of all, small. If the room was a 20x18, had 12 ft. ceilings with a sitting room attached and an extra wet bar on the other side (who doesn't need a wet bar in the bedroom?), then maybe it would fit. However, in your traditional sized master, not so much.

If you need a little help with colors, a white bedspread with cream accents can create a timeless look. The neutral bedding allows for a little pop of color with pillows, throw blankets and artwork. As expensive as the 20-year-old custom drapes were, they are antiquated and need to be removed. It would be more preferred to have just the blinds to incorporate some calm natural light.

In the master bath, all personal items should be removed. Meaning all toothbrushes, hair brushes, medicines, and any other assorted hygiene products. I suggest having white hand towels with fresh flowers. A candle with a spa like sent is a great idea as well. Make sure the bathroom is super clean, I'm talking, your mother is coming from out of town and staying with you clean. Clean the toilet thoroughly and be sure to keep the seat down, even if it's clean. Things get built up over time so grab a magic eraser or some barkeepers friend and go to town on the tile, grout, bathtub and anywhere you suspect it needs to be cleaned up.

It is not imperative that you make the closets fully decluttered and staged as you are most likely still living in the house, after all. Buyers understand, but be sure to put away excess items, so it is easy for them to walk in and get an idea of how much the space can hold. In a vacant house, it is a nice touch to have a few articles of clothing hung on the rack, a few shoes strategically placed and a couple of multi-sized wrapped gift bags to provide an extra touch.

A friendly reminder to have valuables removed or locked up. This includes any prescription pills, cash, jewelry, firearms, and any sensitive personal information you might have around the home. Trust that people will do the right thing, but don't make it easy for them if they don't. Any truly priceless items should be removed from the house while it is listed and showings are being held.

The master bedroom is particularly important to buyers. Thus, the room needs extra attention with cleaning and staging. Put away your personal hygiene items, clean and dust thoroughly. Declutter and make sure the buyers feel they can enjoy spending time in their new master suite. Not doing your due diligence in this part of the home, can have a negative effect on an otherwise potential sale of your house.

THE HOUSE AND THE BACKYARD

Moving onto the rest of the house and the backyard. In the remaining bedrooms, you will want to continue to depersonalize, declutter and delight the buyers. Make sure you tackle the kid's rooms and that guest bedroom that has turned into a catch-all storage warehouse. With the kids rooms, buyers understand it will not always be perfectly clean and that you can't get rid of all their toys and personal items. What you can do, is hide toys away in storage containers under the beds, in closets and in plain sight if it helps the kiddos pick up their room quickly for showings. There are times when buyers provide minimal warning with a showing request. Because of this, it is important to have the kids rooms at a "guest in 20 minutes" stage. Honestly, every space in your house should be kept this way while showings are occurring.

Most of the time you will need to pack up or give toys away to allow the future homeowners to really see the size of the room and not be overwhelmed by the sheer volume of toys. I mean, how many toys do these kids really need? I say this as I step over a Peppa Pig kingdom in the hallway to get to my kitchen.

Regarding paint colors, I usually suggest leaving the paint color the same unless it's just plain ugly or if the walls are in rough condition. If it's a family home, most likely the buyers will have a family with kids that will love the superman themed bedroom or a little girl for the pink bedroom (there is always...a pink bedroom... always). Most buyers will understand that a room or two can be painted fairly inexpensively, so I suggest leaving the paint colors and providing a credit to the buyer at closing if it is a concern for them. If it is not a family home, and the extra bedroom is an office, guest bedroom and so forth, well, even better! Less items to declutter. It's okay to have an empty bedroom if the rest of the place is staged. Actually, if you are renting furniture and decorations, you really only need to stage the living room, kitchen and master bedroom. If there is money left over then you can spend some money on the back patio, dining room, game room and a bedroom or two.

Game rooms and media rooms need to be set up so that the buyers can really see themselves hanging out with family and friends watching the game or a movie all together. Movie posters in the media room are uber cliché, but so wonderful in providing the home movie theater feel. Furniture, sound systems, and electronics are often negotiated in the sale of the home, especially if you have a sweet set up so be sure to have the discussion of what items are off limits and which ones are negotiable as buyers will ask (I like your house…but only if it comes with that limited edition Russian nesting doll set…). You can have these kinds of items excluded, but trust me, if that chandelier really means that much to you, then take it down and replace it before you put your home on the market and save yourself a lot of grief.

Moving to the backyard, it will either be a great selling feature, or will need to be minimized in the marketing of your house. What I mean is, if you have a great set up with a custom patio cover, outdoor TV, firepit, custom landscaping and a built-in homebrew kegerator, then by all means, decorate and play up the outdoor living space you've created! But if you just have the basic builder grade patio, no trees and no landscaping, and no view, and your lawn hasn't been mowed in three weeks, then you need to make sure that the backyard is not made a selling feature. Buyers will want to see the size of the yard but will understand that it looks like all the other yards they have seen. I do love a custom patio & outdoor living area but be careful about how much money you put into backyard upgrades. Most appraisers don't give much value for outdoor upgrades (except for pools but even then it's usually not half of what they cost to install).

For homes closer to a central business district (downtown), a sodded yard becomes a highly desirable feature for buyers with pets and is a selling feature that should be a top marketing element. Some homes and townhomes built closer to downtown don't often have much of a yard so laying down some crushed granite or the ever more popular, high quality AstroTurf®, is a fantastic idea. The AstroTurf® provides the feel of grass with no mud and pets can do their business and clean up just needs a grocery bag and a quick spray of the hose. The trick here is to think "different" but also be cost effective.

It may be worth having a professional lawn service for a month or so to help get the yard in its best shape. Make sure to have the trees trimmed, especially if they are rubbing against the house. Flowerbeds should be mulched with black mulch, weeds removed, and some fresh annuals added for color. If you have a nice patio set, clean it up and add some new cushions with some color. A simple herb garden in a low profile pot is a great useful centerpiece to any outdoor table.

Spending a few hours of your weekend or having a professional come, to power wash the driveway, patio, and siding of the house (only if necessary) provides an inexpensive means of freshening up the exterior. Make sure to clean BOTH sides of the windows and remove any dirt in the window sills. Gutters should not have plants growing in them...so make sure to clean them out.

Continue to think of small things to add value to your house that don't cost a lot of money other than your time and a little elbow grease. The little details you focus on will help provide buyers with a great sense that the house has been well-cared for. Be careful not to over improve the exterior portion of your house as again, most appraisers don't provide much value to the overall sale of the house. And finally, make sure your house stands out from the "sameness" of the competition through cleaning, pops of color, and little "wow" moments that delight the buyer and attached them to your house.

ACTION PLAN:

- Meet with a professional stager to help prepare your home to look its best (think first date) and to stand out from the competition.

- Declutter, depersonalize and delight buyers with great furniture and decorations.

- Put away valuables or remove them from the house to prevent them wandering off.

- Check out the "Home Staging Checklist" on page 145 to prepare your home and get ready to work with your staging professional

AMAZING PROPERTY SHOTS
STEP 5: PROFESSIONAL PHOTOGRAPHY & VIRTUAL TOURS

> *"Photography helps people to see."*
> *– Berenice Abbott*

MARKETING IS ABOUT STANDING OUT in an overwhelming crowd of "sameness." A quick search on your local MLS (Multiple Listing Service – AKA, where real estate agents upload and market the houses for sale) or online property search engine, and you will see a sea of listings with absolutely terrible pictures. A majority of the pictures are taken with the agent's phone and it really shows. Seasoned agents will sometimes still use a point and shoot camera and forget to take off the timestamp, so it looks like they had the photos developed and then scanned in, which is also a real winner.

When you do see a house with professional pictures it just stands out like a purple unicorn in New York City. Even if it's outside the budget or not in your desired location, you almost can't help but click to see more. That's exactly what you want for your house!

Some house listings will have the same picture 6 times (6 pictures is the required minimum for the MLS in our area), some will just have a few pictures of a really nice house, but the pictures are so awful that it really turns you off from exploring them. My favorite pictures are when the owners are nonchalantly on the couch watching TV. I mean, really? You couldn't even get up and turn off the TV for two minutes while pictures of your house are taken so you can sell it and move on with your life? It makes me laugh on the outside, but cry a lot on the inside.

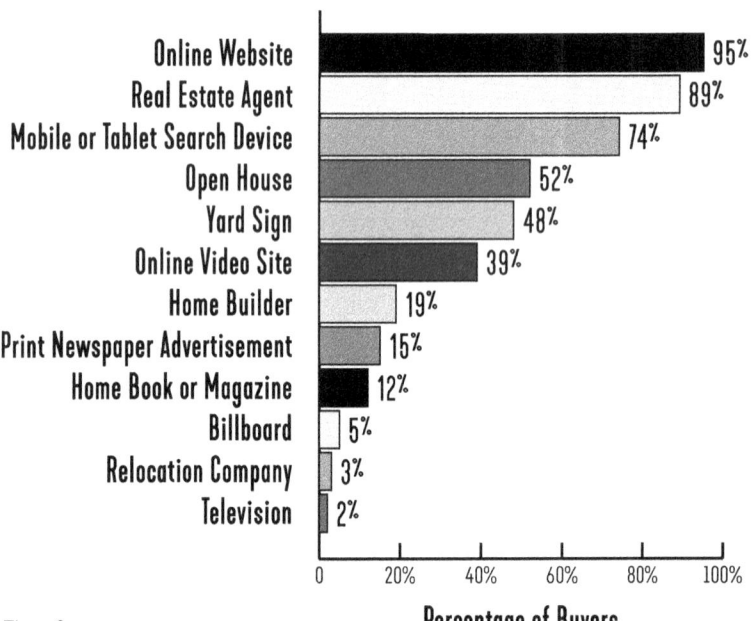

Figure 3

Take a look! Don't take my word for it, just do a five minute search and you will see what I'm talking about. Even some multi-million dollar homes have terrible pictures! So let's keep it simple, stand out in a crowd from the other homes for sale, purchase high quality photos from a professional.

STEP #5:
TAKE AMAZING PROPERTY PICTURES

The National Association of Realtors® conducts an annual study[6] on the avenues buyers use to search for properties. Since 2007, the most used source was the internet at 88% of respondents, and that number has only increased in subsequent years.

As you can see in Figure 3 to the left, the top avenues used by buyers are the internet, a real estate agent, a yard sign and open house. So, if over 95% of buyers are online, doesn't it make sense to have a strong online presence? Unequivocally it does! It's just about a waste of time to focus on newspaper & magazine ads as a top marketing strategy if that only reaches 12% & 5% of buyers. You can get more views with your online marketing, for less money and receive better results.

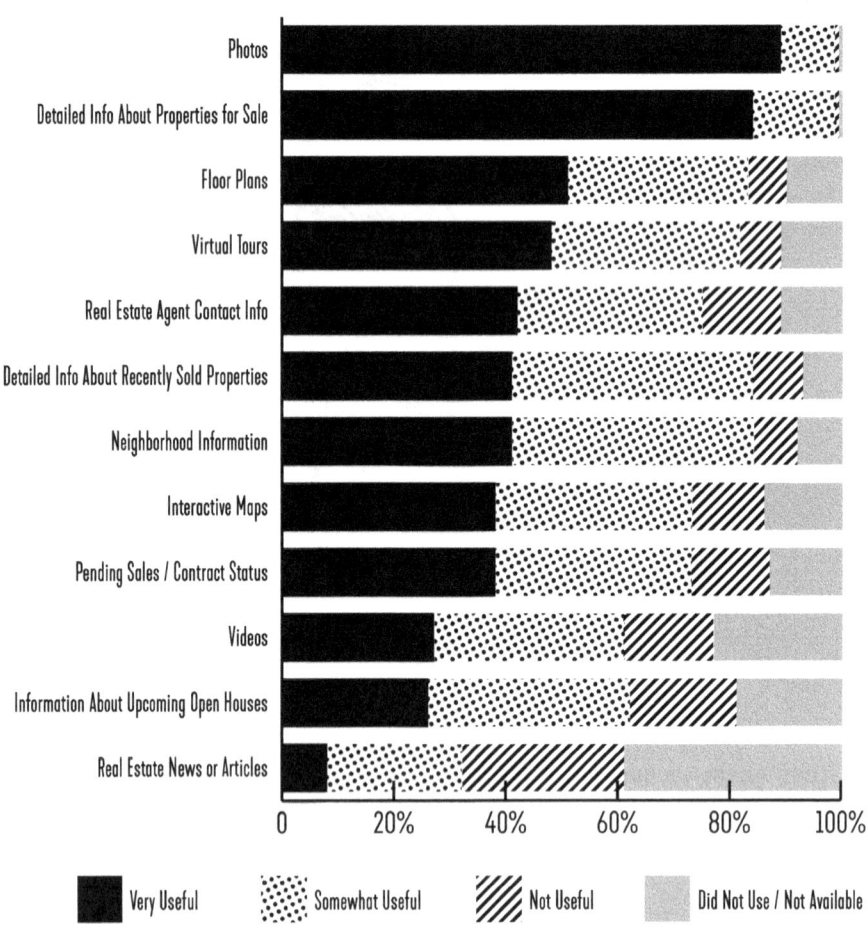

Figure 4

While print marketing is not dead (I still do a good amount of it), it's best to maximize your home's online presence because that is where almost all buyers are spending their time. In terms of real estate marketing, most print ads just direct a buyer to an online location. The National Association of Realtors® completed another study[6] in which they asked, *"What do buyers deem very useful in their online search?"* (Figure 4)

It's no surprise that photos are at the top of the list followed by property details, virtual tours & floor plans. What this all means is that if you want to have the most effective marketing for the least amount of cost; focus on a great online presence with pictures that stand out, descriptive property details, and a virtual tour that helps buyers better understand the layout. Most real estate search sites have an interactive map search.

Look online at the homes for sale in your neighborhood and you will notice that a vast majority of homes are lacking in the top four features that buyers are looking for:

1) Great Pictures
2) Ample Property Details
3) Floor Plans &
4) Virtual Tours

Often, the homes that have terrible photography, also have minor amounts of property description. These poorly marketed homes, rarely have more details listed about them than how many bedrooms & bathrooms are within the house. They all however, have a general call to action, "don't miss this one!" They should have taken their own advice when it comes to marketing as they missed the boat completely.

When scrolling through homes online, an average person will notice a difference in the quality of pictures taken instantly, and I'll bet my last dollar that they are spending more time on the homes that have amazing pictures and have been staged. These professionally photographed and staged homes simply look better. The homes appear to be in their best shape. This translates to potential buyers spending more time looking at and considering these homes and listings.

Great pictures drive more clicks to your listing. More clicks means more buyers are seeing your house, and that results in more tours. More tours and showings result in offers. We all know offers make you, and your agent for that matter, happy. An accepted offer also means you don't have to continue showing your house and keeping it immaculately clean.

My team uses a couple of professional photographers and I pick the one with the particular skill set needed for each property. I always make sure to use a HDR photographer. HDR stands for "High-Dynamic-Range" and it basically means that the camera takes multiple pictures of the same image using different exposures and compresses them into a single image. This creates a crisp, bright and stunning image. Some buyers will get frustrated that it doesn't quite look the same in real life, but it represents the home in its best light… literally.

Our pictures are so good, that once I show the homeowner the pictures we have taken of their abode, 70% of the time (yea, I did the math, trust me…I'm a doctor) they will say, "Wow! Is that my house?" It's a great joy to see a homeowner excited about all the hard work they have done getting their house "show ready" and seeing it pay off in stunning pictures for their upcoming listing.

The other important thing to do with these great pictures is to make sure you and your real estate agent are putting the best and most attention grabbing image up front. If all the other homes in the area have an exterior picture of the house as their first image, then I put the totally decked out kitchen as the first picture. Same thing with all interior pictures first, I will put another awesome selling feature upfront, like the inviting back patio, or the master retreat, or the crazy awesome media room. It just needs to be something different in the sea of "sameness" to grab the buyers attention to which they are intrigued enough to click and spend time looking at your house.

One thing I love to do is to take our pictures at twilight, this is just before the sun comes up or sets as there is still a little sunlight but no harsh shadows. It also makes the exterior pictures pop! If the sky isn't particularly beautiful at the time of the shoot, then we have the photographer switch out to a sky that is crazy pink, or fiery red, or has some beautiful billowing clouds in the background. This creates an image that is so unique, so enticing that buyers not even looking in your home's pricing and area will want to click it.

Now that we have great pictures of your house and a killer first image, you and your agent want to make sure that your first six pictures on the MLS are the best ones. I do this for a couple of reasons:

1. Some real estate websites and syndicated apps will only put up 5-10 pictures.
2. We want your house to put its best features up front.
3. Buyers are impatient and won't look through all 43 images we upload and will stop after the first few if they don't see something they like.

It is for these reasons, that it kills me when agents upload ten pictures of just the front of the house. This causes the buyer, and myself, to click through them all to see if the living room is the layout that my particular buyer is looking for. I get a little impatient as well, I guess, add it to the list of self improvement items I need to work on.

After focusing on getting the best photos possible, positioning the best and most wonderful pictures up front, making sure the house stands out from the "sameness" in the neighborhood, it then becomes time for the next item of business. It is a good idea for the agent to set up a 3D Virtual Tour for the house. The eye catching pictures draw buyers in but, the images are only 2D. Buyers are unable to understand how the house flows from room to room. When a 3D virtual tour is made and available on the MLS listing, buyers are able to move from room to room, change their view to 360°, and can see if the layout of the house is what they are looking for.

I find that the virtual tours helps to eliminate some of the "Looky Lou's" who want to see if it has the kitchen floor plan they are looking for or if the kitchen is open enough to the living area for their tastes. With a 3D Virtual Tour, it allows them to see your house as if they were walking through it but without having to waste your time with a tour if "that feature" is a deal breaker to them.

The 3D Virtual Tour also has a "dollhouse feature" that creates a digital dollhouse of your house. This feature enables you to spin around in the home virtually, and see the house online as if it were a mini home. Many 3D Virtual Tour programs have this and your agent and professional photographer can make sure this is included. While it's not necessarily going to sell your house, it's pretty dang cool. You'll remember that floor plans are number three on the list of items buyers find most helpful and if you don't have the original builder floor plan, then the 3D dollhouse view can be a great modern replacement.

Don't skimp on the pictures! Make sure you have amazing images to help your house stand out from the competition. Include a 3D Virtual Tour as well to help buyers better understand the layout and flow of the house.

ACTION PLAN:

- Don't be a cheapskate, make sure you home is shown in its best light, pay for professional pictures.

- Get a 3D Virtual Tour of your house.

STAND OUT FROM THE COMPETITION
STEP 6: WHAT MAKES YOUR HOME UNIQUE?

*"In a crowded marketplace,
fitting in is a failure.
In a busy marketplace,
not standing out is being invisible."*

– Seth Godin

WHY DID YOU BUY THE HOUSE you are living in? What made it stick out from all the other houses you toured? What do you love most about your house?

Your answer to these questions will usually be the top features used in the marketing of your house. The reason you fell in love with your house will most likely be the same reason your buyer falls in love with the house.

To get the old grey matter working, here are some examples: beautiful, tall windows that let in tons of natural light for an inviting feeling, an awesome patio that is great for enjoying coffee in the morning or a cocktail in the evening, a great cul-de-sac that has a bunch of kids on it for your kids to play with, or a gameroom that is large but closed off enough to let the kids play without disturbing guests downstairs. It doesn't have to be dramatic, many times it's just the little things that make a house stand out enough for you and the future homeowner to buy it.

One client of mine, bought their house because it backed up to a wooded area. They felt a sense of privacy and enjoyed beauty of the mature trees rather than someone else's backyard. Another client, bought their house because the builder utilized the space in the house well. It was important to them to have as little "wasted space" as possible whereas, many of my other clients loved vaulted two story ceilings. One client bought their house because the layout allowed them to section off a portion of their house for their dogs to live in. Each house and each buyer is different. The trick is to match your house to the right buyer.

STEP #6:
DETERMINE WHAT MAKES YOUR HOME UNIQUE

It doesn't really matter how important or seemingly insignificant the features are that created enough value to give you the confidence to purchase the house when you did. Think deeply about all the reasons you really love your house, brainstorm by writing them down on paper and share that with your real estate professional. Again, you want to stand out from the "sameness" crowd. Even the seemly small features will set you apart. This is especially helpful when selling your tract home (a basic floor plan and level of upgrades a builder builds throughout a neighborhood). Any positive difference will help with standing out, quite literally breaking the mold.

Buyers purchase homes for many reasons. At the end of the day, it comes down to value. Does your house provide more "value" to them than the other homes on the market? Think of all the other active homes on the market as your competition. Your goal is to stand out among the other area listings, to win the hearts and minds of the buyers actively looking.

Pointing out what you and your family love about the house, will help to encourage buyers to feel the same way. It is all about emotion. It is important to stand out from the beginning, not 60 days into your listing. Standing out above the rest helps to receive multiple offers, and fast, because buyers see something different, they see what you see, and want to love the house just as you have. Your goal, after all, is to sell the house, receive multiple offers, and go under contract. To do that, we need to create value in the buyer's mind.

I want to suggest to you that, if possible, tour the other houses on the market with similar attributes to yours, and see how they compare. Put on your "buyer's hat" and see their house through the eyes of a buyer. Does the home have an inviting feeling when you first walk in? How is the layout, is it open and welcoming? What does the house initially smell like? Do you see many items that need to be repaired or does it feel like it's "Move-In-Ready?" If updates and repairs have been made, does it appear professionally done or as if the homeowner did it themselves? As you walk through, make note of your buyer's tally, and by that, I mean the running tally in your head of all the costs of repairs and/or updates you notice that need to be completed.

If you see an updated kitchen but older appliances, subtract from the listing price what you believe would cost to replace the appliances with something modern. If you see siding that is rotting, a roof on its last leg, and cracks in the drywall, then know that any other buyer for that house is subtracting the cost of the repairs that need to be made from the sales price. But if you tour a house in your neighborhood that is your competition, and as you walk through you don't have a running tally of things to repair or update, then it is probably in great condition and potential buyers will notice as well.

When a buyer walks through your house, what do you think their running tally of repair costs and updates will be? If they are subtracting the cost of new paint, new wood flooring to replace the ratty carpet and a full remodel to the kitchen, then know the value they think your house is worth is going to be much less than you value it. It's tough to be honest with yourself as to how your house compares to the competition.

Now, getting back to value, there are three different ways to add value and they are no secret. The first one is condition. Is your house in better condition than your competition? As we discussed in the previous chapters, getting your house into top shape will help you sell for more money, faster. This is because there are a large portion of buyers that will pay extra for a home that is "Move-In-Ready." That running tally I mentioned? Yea, for a buyer to perceive a "Move-In-Ready" home, that "tally" needs to be as close to zero as possible. If not the other way around, to have buyers saying, "I can't believe they priced the home this way with how great a condition it's in!"

Next, and usually the biggest determining factor, is price. You can add value by pricing your house less than the other comparable houses in the market. If you are honest with yourself, and your house is just a little under the level of finishes of the competition, then pricing it lower is a great way to provide value to the buyer. If all the homes are at $750,000 that are comparable to yours and you list at $699,000, buyers will see the value in your house because it is a good deal. Who doesn't want a good deal? I don't immediately like to go to this option but sometimes it's in the best interests of a homeowner. We will talk more about that in chapter 7 on pricing.

Finally, the last item to provide value is location. A home residing on a cul-de-sac, with a park a block away, is going to sell for a higher price and more quickly than a comparable home on a busy street or a house with commercial real estate behind it. A house a few blocks away from the commuter rail will be more desirable than one miles from the nearest train stop. You can't really do much with the location, unless you are in a tiny home (AKA mobile home), and so it is best to focus on what you can control; the condition and price of your house. Just be glad you don't have a composting toilet.

But, wait! There's more!

There is a 4th wild card, and that is marketing! One of my most important jobs as a real estate professional is to market your house like crazy so that we get as many interested buyers to tour as possible. Your job is to take care of the condition and the pricing, and I market like it is my job...well, as your real estate agent, it is my job. If a home is priced too high or its in terrible condition or if it backs up to a business of ill repute, then no amount of marketing will get a house sold. Some sellers I wanted to help have been so out of touch with the market on pricing and condition that even if I were to put their house on the front page of the largest local newspaper, it still wouldn't sell. So, marketing does help sell homes but in conjunction with pricing it correctly in relation to the condition.

Marketing helps to create value in a buyer's mind through perceived benefits, as well as to identify with an owner's story. There is much to discuss on this and we will explore it further in chapter 9. I know, I am such a tease! For now, know that good, quality marketing is crazy important.

Price, condition, location, and marketing are all ways that you as a homeowner can create value in a buyer's mind. Your house will not appeal to all buyers in the market because your house can't be everything to everybody. Some sellers really take offense to buyers not liking their house after they tour, but remember it is not you, it's them, they were just not the right fit. It is extremely important to imagine who your most likely buyer will be. If you are zoned to great schools, have a large backyard and an open living area, there is a good chance your most likely buyer will have a family. If your house is close to downtown, has a minimalist design, no backyard and high-end finishes, then your most likely buyer is probably a couple looking to have a quick commute, entertain often and enjoy the walkability of the city.

Whoever is your most likely buyer will determine how you focus on staging and marketing the house to meet that buyer's particular needs. That is not to say a family can't buy a super sleek and modern house close to downtown, it's just not as likely because they are interested in and need different things.

In online marketing, they call this your "avatar" (not the really tall blue people from the movie). Your "avatar" is the profile of your most likely buyer. If you have a one bedroom condo close to downtown, then you do a little research and find that your most likely buyer will be a young professional just starting their career and looking to own a place of their own close to their office. Begin to think about what that young professional is looking for. In addition to a nice home, what might their lifestyle be? How can your house contribute to that?

What if you own a multi-million-dollar house in one of the finner neighborhoods of your area? What is your avatar? Is it a young family? Is it two empty nesters? Is it a young internet tycoon wanting to make a splash by purchasing the most expensive house in the city? Whoever it is, think about what they need. Think about what they value. What organizations they may be apart of? Ask yourself, "what country clubs, gyms, or bowling leagues are they members of?" Then work backwards to meet their needs, so that buying your house makes perfect sense to them.

The last thing to think about in this chapter is the fringe buyer. These are buyers out in the marketplace that are looking for a specific kind of property that rarely comes up. For example, I had a home I sold in less than a week from marketing at an open house because the seller had converted the garage into a separate casita with its own kitchen, laundry, and dining area. The home had previously been listed for 6 months without a buyer. The seller did a few updates that I suggested, but when I began marketing it, I made sure to promote the casita (which is Spanish for...the casita...actually it means little house, I digress). I used this casita as an important part of the marketing and it paid off. The buyers had been looking for a home with separate living quarters for over two years. Almost all the other buyers I showed the casita to, were turned off that it didn't have a garage. However, the right, and eventual buyers couldn't have been happier. They had found what they were looking for. All of this was possible because the marketing I did highlighted a unique feature of the home, and in a positive light.

Another client said they looked for the right house for over a year due to their very specific qualifications. They needed to have two master bedrooms, one upstairs and one down. Well, the owner of the house they purchased had added a 2nd floor with a huge master bedroom and bathroom but left the original 3 bedrooms downstairs intact, so it was a little strange for some buyers, but perfect for them.

I also had a property that was flipped by an investor; it was beautifully redone with tons of tours but no offers after a couple of months. The feedback was all positive except that the house wasn't in the best area. After a couple of months of no offers, we terminated the listing and re-listed it on the MLS but this time focused on the extended "shed" that was the garage and called it a workshop. The garage wasn't finished at all and, to me, felt like a dungeon, but it was rather large at around 1,500 sq.ft. This change in perspective and play on words worked. We received a good offer in just a couple of weeks. The new homeowner loved woodworking and needed the extra space for his tools and projects. Embrace your home's uniqueness and let it stand out so that not only are you an option for "normal" buyers, but that you can potentially hit those "fringe buyers" that are waiting for just the right house.

Of course, we don't want to make your house so strange that it dwindles your pool of potential buyers to that of a mere puddle (see what I did there?). Your house should appeal to a motivated set of buyers who are most likely to purchase your house while keeping in mind potential fringe buyers.

So, who is your avatar?

ACTION PLAN

- Create a list of all the features that made you fall in love with your house and make in an important marketing feature

- Tour other comparable homes in your market (your competition) to see how you stand out and if buyers will perceive your house to be a good "value."

- Think about your "avatar," what do they want, need and how does your house fit their lifestyle?

- Consider any features that "fringe buyers" would stop their marathon search to buy your house.

THE PRICE IS RIGHT
STEP 7: PRICING YOUR HOUSE

*"The buyer is entitled to a bargain.
The seller is entitled to a profit.
So there is a fine margin in between
where the price is right."*

– Conrad Hilton

HUMANS ARE SUCH EMOTIONAL CREATURES. I deal with emotions everyday. Yes, my own emotions, but I am speaking about the emotions from all parties in a transaction. Pricing a house is such an emotional decision that it can be difficult for some clients to accept the facts of what the market is revealing. Here is an example of a conversation I have had more than once:

Me: "Mr. & Mrs. Seller, your house is worth $275,000. This is because we can see from the market comparables, that there are 4 homes with the exact same floor plan, with the same updates and on the same street...that sold yesterday..."

Mr. Seller: "But we added gutters to the garage, painted the entire house, and it's our house so buyers will see how special it is. We want to list for $399,000 and we will be insulted if anyone offers less!"

I get it. It's your house. It's where you have great memories with family and friends. It's where you brought your first child home. It's where you scrimped and saved enough money just to get enough for the down payment. It's where you had the last Christmas together with Grandma before she passed away. There are some special memories this house has been apart of. These are memories you and your family will always cherish.

The honest truth is most buyers don't really care. Great memories won't make the house worth any more to potential buyers than the house down the street. Those memories are yours, and not the buyers. They do care, however, if you took care of the home. Remember, at the end of the day, buyers want to get a great deal.

Another emotional attachment I have to work through, is most homeowners want to get back every dollar they put into the house. "Well, we spent $25,000 on the kitchen remodel, $7,000 on new wood flooring, $11,000 on new exterior siding and gutters, and I just put in new mulch for $35.71. So I'll need to sell my house for $43,035.71 more than I paid for it or we are not selling." Although I understand where Mr. Seller is coming from, that is not how a buyer sees a home, nor how the real estate market works.

It is a tough conversation to have, discussing that not every dollar a homeowner puts into their house gets a 1:1 return. In some areas and in some hot markets, you can get a fantastic return on such updates, but not always. Knowing the difference, and where your house falls, is why you should talk with your real estate professional before starting any major updates. It is common for mechanical systems, such as the HVAC, water heater, and electrical box to not get much return on investment at all. If that was the case, all sellers would have them shiny and new, but in reality, they usually don't add much equity. This is why, when you see flipped houses, many flippers will address mostly cosmetic updates because it provides the greatest return on their investment. This is not to say you shouldn't address these items. A poorly maintained house will scare buyers away, if not initially, then right after the inspection report comes in.

Anyone selling a house will have a difficult time rationally determining what it is worth. We all make decisions emotionally and justify logically (particularly real estate agents selling their personal homes). One client I had was dead set that his house worth $40,000 more than a comparable property because he had "two trees in the front yard and they only had one." You laugh, but you know deep down you have had similar thoughts.

STEP #7:
PRICE YOUR HOUSE TO SELL

When discussing pricing with your real estate professional, try to take the emotion out of it. You need to understand some of the greater market forces affecting home values as well as what is going on specifically in your neighborhood. A hot seller's market with an strong economy will drive home values up while a buyer's market (lots of home inventory with little demand) will have you competing for buyers by dramatically reducing your price.

The Comparable Market Analysis (CMA) will direct you to a small price range that your house is worth, and usually can be adjusted up or down depending upon the value your house provides compared to the competition. A home's value is about the numbers and its condition, not the emotion of it.

There is a direct relationship between sales price and condition. The better condition the home is in, the higher price it can command. The worse the condition is, the lower the price it will command (a novel concept, am I right?). To help a homeowner understand the relationship, I'll often draw a simple line and put in a range of home conditions: original home, average "lived-in" home, and HGTV ready home.

An "original home" is a house that doesn't have any updates but is well maintained. Sometimes, in a buyers market, it is a foreclosure or a "fixer upper." An average home is your normal, everyday lived in home that the homeowner has tried to maintain and update over the years, but isn't the most stylish and may still have some un-updated aspects. An HGTV ready home is your "top of the line" house with the most current trends, high-end finishes, perfect decorations, and on point design.

Next, I'll ask the seller's to put a mark on the spectrum where they think there home is currently.

| Original Home | Average Home | HGTV Ready Home |

Then I'll take two comparable homes that sold in their neighborhood in the last year or less and place them on the range. I first show the "original home" pictures to provide them with a base of the lowest comparable home sold. Then, I will show them the best property that has all the high-end updates, and usually has more square feet than their house, as well as amenities like; a pool, outdoor kitchen, media room, sauna, etc. I use this fully furnished home as the top end example.

I will then place the two home's prices on the line that they marked previously to see how it lines up.

| Original Home | Average Home | HGTV Ready Home |
| $280,000 | $360,000 | $420,000 |

Sometimes they will be offended, and say that it's worth more than the max value on the spectrum. Then, I know that I am dealing with an owner that needs to be brought back down to Earth on pricing. Most of the time, in my experience, this exercise provides a moment of clarity for the owners because they start to understand the relationship between price and condition.

If they don't like the price then I say, "no problem, all you have to do is get your home in HGTV Dream Home condition and you can get the price you desire." I then go through the things they would need to do to get up to the top end of the market. Usually it is not feasible, but I do create a game plan to help them win. This is in order to help them to maximize their home's value with little cost. The key is, they...and you...have to be willing to do the work.

After we have a talk on the relationship between the condition of their house and price, we end at their eventual sales price range. I prefer to give homeowners a narrowed price range that their house should sell for and coach them in deciding what is best for them and their family. It usually consists of 3 starting prices:

1. The Low Starting Price: "The Sell Your House Fast and Hope For Multiple Offers to Drive Up The Value" (Ex. $280,000)

2. The Medium Starting Price: "The Middle of the Road and What Your Home is Most Likely Worth" (Ex. $360,000)

3. Maximum Starting Price: "The Top of the Market" (Ex. $420,000)

Let's go into each of these and discuss why a homeowner would want to choose from them. With the low starting price, it doesn't guarantee a sale, but it sure should get a lot of attention. If there are a large number of buyers for the price point, then we usually see a lot of showings ("showings" refer to buyers touring a house). With the high level of interest, we hope for multiple offers and that bids the price up. This strategy works well at lower price points, but less so for luxury markets, whatever those price points may be in your area.

The Medium Starting Price is usually where most homeowners list their homes. After reviewing the CMA, it makes most sense to get the most for the house but not spend a long time on the market.

Finally, the Maximum Starting Price is pretty much where you think your house will be, but rarely hits this number. This is close to the absolute max your house can sell for in the current market. At this price, you are still in the market, but your pool of potential buyers is tremendously small, and your house can stay on the market for an extended period. The condition of the house needs to be immaculate with the absolute best updates. The home needs to be staged out of its mind like it is ready for a editorial photoshoot. It's not quite "HGTV Dream Home" quality, as discussed previously, but it's up there.

You will notice that I said these are the 3 different STARTING prices and not selling prices. As a real estate professional who assists with buying and selling homes every day, I review the market, do a comparisons report, add and subtract value depending upon the condition of your home, and study market trends. With all of that work and research, I still don't know for an absolute fact what your house will sell for. The market is the ultimate decision maker on what a home is worth.

Market Value: (Text book definition) what a willing buyer will pay for a home and what a willing seller will sell a home for.

The $140,000 spread in price is a bit much, but it does illustrate that buyers still perceive value on condition, location, and price (and marketing!). My clients tend to focus on the higher end of the market by completing purposeful updates that provide an ROI (Return on Investment). Meaning, beautifully stage the house and market it like crazy. The challenge with focusing on the upper end of the market value is that the pool of buyers is limited, and homeowners use the starting price as their anchor point. "But we were listed at $599k, we can't drop to $560k, that's too low!" While a homeowner may have in their head what they will make from the sale of the home at top price, it doesn't matter if the house doesn't receive any offers.

We read the "tea leaves" so to speak of what the market is telling us about each house. The most important factors to consider are:

1. What feedback buyers are consistently providing about the house.

2. Which comparable houses have gone under contract while your house has been on the market and the likely reasons (price, condition, location or marketing).

3. What the internet traffic looks like, the number of showings per week and the number of offers, and the offer prices received.

All these factors and more are taken into account when selling a home that has been on the market for a week or more. If you are not even in the ballpark of what the market value is, then buyers won't tour, and they definitely won't send offers close to the listing price.

We review the weekly stats with our homeowners and discuss the marketing activities, the showing feedback, the traffic, and all related info to make sure we are at or close to market value. The National Association of Realtors® has studied home selling numbers for many years and a number that consistently stays true through the ups and downs of the market is that a home will sell within an average of 3% of the list price. That means that a home will most likely sell for 97% of the listing price. Since buyers are always looking for a "deal" they will try to drop the price as low as they can. With that said, getting into the "market value range" can take some price changes and reductions to get to where a buyer will pay 97% of the current list price. (Yun6).

I've had houses that were listed at one price for a couple of months and with a price drop or two, interest in them takes off like crazy! One helpful series of stats my team in our area has access to, is the number of showings other homes in the area are receiving. It doesn't provide stats for a particular house, unless it's our listing, but I can see the showings by week and by price point for a particular area or zip code. It's very telling to see houses in the same zip code priced at $875,000 to $900,000 get 13% more showings than those $900,000 to $925,000 (less than a 3% difference). While it may seem inconsequential, it can make a world of difference in a buyer's mind and a buyer's budget.

CSS Showings Stats

Price Range	Number of Showings	% at Price Level	Montly Average	Weekly Average	Showings Per Listing
740,000 to 760,000	5	3.5	0.9	0.2	2.5
760,000 to 780,000	15	10.5	2.6	0.6	5
780,000 to 800,000	43	30.1	7.4	1.7	5.4
800,000 to 820,000	6	4.2	1	0.2	3
820,000 to 840,000	4	2.8	0.7	0.2	4
840,000 to 860,000	14	9.8	2.4	0.6	7
860,000 to 880,000	0	0	0	0	0
880,000 to 900,000	24	16.8	4.1	0.9	6
900,000 to 920,000	2	1.4	0.3	0.1	2
920,000 to 940,000	13	9.1	2.2	0.5	6.5
940,000 to 960,000	17	11.9	2.9	0.7	8.5
Total	143	100	2.9		

Figure 5

Did I tell you that selling a house is an emotional event? Well, so is buying, and a great property can become victim to a buyer's emotions. For example, have you ever seen a great house listed for sale for a good price in your neighborhood that sat around for entirely too long? In your own mind, you probably thought, "I wonder what's wrong with it?" The answer is usually, "absolutely nothing" other than the home is overpriced for its condition.

This shred of doubt however, does get the potential buyers thinking something is wrong, even before they tour, and this mentality changes their attitude and perception. When walking into a home that has been on the market a while and hasn't sold, buyers are thinking, "What's wrong with it," and "Why hasn't anyone else bought it yet?" Buyers are on the defensive as if something is going to jump out and literally attack them. No one wants to be blindsided. In this instance, I usually say that it has been on the market a while only because "the house is just waiting for the perfect buyers like you." I can be a cheeseball, I know.

It is a school of fish mentality…and we all have it. We all swim, close together mind you, in the same direction or another. If other buyers are interested and touring a home, so are we. If they are not, then we are not either. A home on the market too long makes a buyer wary because no one else has purchased it. On the other end, a hot property with lots of tours and few days on the market gets buyers excited, particularly when they know other people are interested. "Someone else wants that house, so it must be pretty good" thinks the buyer. They rationalize that because other people like a house that it validates their feelings for wanting to put an offer on it. This social proof is why homes that receive an offer (even after many days on market) will often receive a second or multiple offers shortly after.

You may not want to hear this, but homes that stay on the market longer sell consistently for less money than homes priced well to begin with. Take a look at the graph in Figure 6 on the next page.

Figure 6

Zillow Research found that homes that sold relatively quick for the market, sold within 1% of the listing price[5]. Homes that were on the market around two months, sold around a 5% drop from the listing price, and homes listed for the longest amount of time (11 months on average) sold at a 12% drop from their listing price. You can see that over time, a homeowner gets more desperate. The "What's wrong with it?" question pops in the buyer's head, and it equates to a lower sales price.

Using the "Max Starting Price" strategy typically leads to longer days on market because the pool of buyers at the top end of the market is smaller. It also takes longer because in a seller's mind they have anchored a price to their house. Often, after I do a large price drop, my clients and I will get an even lower offer. "Don't they know I just dropped the price $50,000!" Yes, it is frustrating, however, if the market is telling us that it is overpriced then a large drop can begin to get you into the right market value. That doesn't mean, however, it will sell for the new reduced price.

I use anchoring a lot when I am negotiating offers that I have submitted for buyer clients. I will start with a low price and work up from there. I know we are not likely to get an accepted contract for a lowball offer, but I also know my buyer clients are not going to overpay market value for the home. It becomes a back and forth between the real estate professionals and clients on both sides. I'll come back often to that starting price and say, "see how much we have come up from our original offer price, my clients are being very generous with coming up to $(insert number here) amount of dollars." Hopefully the back and forth eventually leads to a signed home under contract. That is afterall the goal, a sold home at a price that both parties are happy with or at least stomach.

As the current homeowner and seller, be careful if you choose to start at the higher end of the market for your listing price. Placing your house on the higher end, especially without the updates and repairs to warrant a higher price, can be extremely difficult to sell. Listing on the higher end also tends to create an unrealistic picture of what a final sales price will be. This makes it hard for an owner to emotionally distance themselves from being attached to selling for anything less than the listed price. These homes also tend not to move very quickly and homeowners get frustrated that their house won't sell. This makes the entire process more painful for everyone involved.

Just about any house can sell, it just takes the right price. With a higher end pricing strategy, I usually build in scheduled price reductions in the marketing calendar. These price drops are usually conditional. Such as not having 10 showings in the first 30 days, then the sellers will drop the price $40,000. If there are not 25 showings and one offer in the next 60 days then the sellers and will drop $10,000.

These conditional price reductions help because it is an objective number in which we can compare to other homes selling in the area. If I am seeing 10-15 tours, I know that this usually leads to at least 1 offer, then it's a good barometer. In a hot market, if you have 10 showings in a week and no offers then you are priced outside the market. One property I listed had 43 showings in a week along with a packed open house and yet it took all 43 tours to get an offer. Make sure you are reading the "tea leaves" so that you are not being unrealistic with your listing price.

When determining your pricing strategy, it is important to consider the price at which the appraiser will likely value your house. If you do choose the Maximum Pricing Strategy and your house does receive a full price offer, it doesn't mean you can take it to the bank just yet. If your buyer is financing the purchase of your house (aka getting a loan), then the bank or lending company will require a 3rd party appraisal. This is where an independent person, and appraiser, "objectively" looks at the comparable homes sold in the market and determines its worth based on adding and subtracting value for differences between them. This is very similar to what we did with the CMA in chapter 1, but with an exceptional level of detail.

The appraiser looks to "sandwich" the house between at least three recently sold homes. They usually use homes that have sold within the past three to six months, but they can go back further depending on the speed and location of the market. When they "sandwich" the house they look for a comparable home that is in better condition and has sold for a higher price, a home that is a less updated and sold for less, and a home that is as similar in price, condition, size and sales price to the subject house.

The appraiser will then adjust the three homes based upon their updates and features. The appraiser will look for homes with similar features and level of updates. However, if the subject property has a finished basement or a beautiful outdoor kitchen and patio, and the homes the appraiser is using to compare are lacking similar updates, then the appraiser will assign a value for that upgrade and add it to the three comparable home's price to even it out. If the subject property has less living space than a comparable home, an appraiser will assign a dollar/square foot value and multiply for each square foot that is different.

Example: The subject property is 2,100 sq. ft., a comparable home: 2,200 sq. ft., and the difference is 100 sq. ft. Here, the appraiser believes the adjustment value for the price range is $40/sq. ft. Therefore, off the bat, the subject home is $4,000 less than the value of the comparable home. This process helps to better compare "apples to apples". It isn't always the case that an appraiser will be comparing homes of the exact same floor plan and square footage, it happens, but not everyday. Thus, finding the most similar homes to your house is the best bet. An appraiser will put each house on a scale to evaluate the differences, just like in this example with a difference of 100 sq. ft, and add and subtract value to make them equal. The appraiser does what they can to put all the comparable homes on a level playing field, as if they were the same home.

Okay, so back to our discussion on how appraisals affect the top dollar you can sell your house for. If a buyer's offer of $350,000 is accepted and later the appraisal comes back at $325,000, then the bank will only loan the buyer up to $325,000. This is because the bank will not fund a loan for more than what a home is appraised at being worth. From there, both the buyer and seller have a few options:

1. Challenge the appraisal or get a new one. In a room of 10 appraisers you'd get 10 different values on the same house. This can be a frustrating option, but it might be worth the couple hundred bucks for a new appraisal to potential get the raise of the $25,000.

2. The buyer comes up with an additional $25,000 to make up for the difference. This is common in a hot market where home inventory is low.

3. You as the seller drop your price $25,000. I know, ouch! However, this is what typically happens in a transaction.

4. Negotiate with the buyer for for some sort of median where they come up with more cash upfront and you lower the price.

5. Buyer backs out and gets their earnest money returned to them. However, the release of earnest money isn't guaranteed and depends on your state and contract terms.

Low appraisals are common in all markets, even more so in hot markets. Where your area market is currently should trigger a discussion when accepting one of multiple offers. In either case, hot or cold market, a financed buyer will need an appraisal. Alternatively, cash buyers do not require one. This is because they are not taking out a loan, it is their money from the start. If a cash buyer deems a home worth $350,000, and is willing to pay cash at that price, then the home is worth $350,000 to them.

Work with your real estate professional to create a strategy to maximize the sale of your house while keeping the days on the market low. If you have worked with the professionals and followed the suggestions from chapter two, three and four, then you are well on your way to a quick sale without leaving anything on the table.

ACTION PLAN

- You only have control of two aspects in the sale of your home; condition and price.

- Price your home correctly depending upon the strategy you and your real estate professional create.

- Study and know the market statistics.

- Adjust the price as necessary to not stay on the market for an extended period of time

PETS, LAUNDRY & KIDDOS
STEP 8: MAKE YOUR HOME AVAILABLE

"You miss 100% of the shots you don't take."

– Wayne Gretzky

"**WHAT? YOU LET STRANGERS** into your house? And you leave purposefully before they come over? What's wrong with you?" said nobody ever. But if you think about it, it is kinda strange.

Now that you have met with the professionals, created a winning game plan, done the repair and updates necessary, staged it beautifully, set yourself up for the right buyer, it is time to finally get your home on the market. Hurray! The time has finally come!

Your real estate professional will upload your house to the Multiple Listing Service (MLS). This will automatically send out to all the top syndicated real estate websites in the country, like *Zillow*. Yep, even that one you just thought about. These sites are where over 90% of home buyers are looking for their next home. The MLS helps you find the buyers that will pay top market value for you house as well.

To maximize your house on the MLS, your real estate professional will make sure that it is optimized with the best pictures, a 3D virtual tour, the best written description of your house, and positioned perfectly for the most likely buyer. Now, your job is to make sure that you are as flexible as your schedule and family will allow. Making your house available for buyers to tour. Even at only a moment's notice.

STEP #8:
MAKE YOUR HOME AS AVAILABLE AS POSSIBLE FOR TOURS

Allowing random strangers to walk through your house in hopes of them falling in love with it, so that they make an offer, is all part of the process. Whenever you buy a car, you make sure to test drive it, you do your research on its history, and shop the price. It is similar when buying a house, a buyer will visit and do all the research available to them.

When a buyer comes over for a tour, the home needs to be in perfect shape. It would be a shame for you to go through all the trouble of decluttering, doing repairs/updates, cleaning, staging and taking awesome pictures for a buyer to walk in and see something way

less presentable than what the pictures show. I know, I know, I know you have 3 kids, a dog, and a family member that randomly decides to pop over from time to time you must entertain. In spite of all that, remember your goal; selling for top price and not leaving anything on the table. Like all good goals, achieving this one takes diligence and at times, personal sacrifice.

    Your house needs to look its best for every tour as you never know if "the one" will tour that day. It is also important to make your house as accessible as possible, meaning, you don't have too many restrictions on when a tour can happen. It is maddening to have a seller denying showing requests again and again. I like to suggest a couple hours notice be provided by the buyer's agents when they want to schedule a tour, so the home can be tidied up and the owners given the chance to plan where they will escape to. This of course doesn't always happen, but it is what I request of agents wanting to show a house I have listed.

If you are living in the house and you have a crazy weeknight running around to meetings and events, then block all showings that night and don't feel bad. It will go a long way to providing you some sanity and peace of mind. Everything else in life may be crazy, but at least you don't have to stress about getting the house in perfect order for a showing on that day. Try to keep this to a minimum in the early days of your time on the market, as that is when most tours are likely to happen and is your best chance to get an offer.

Kids are the best. I have two of them myself, but man, they can destroy a house in no time flat. Working with your family to keep the house in top shape needs teamwork so it would be a good idea to have a process of items that need to be cleaned and to be sure to go over that process with all family in the house.

1. All toys placed in toy boxes.
2. Dirty clothes placed in the bin and clean clothes put away.
3. Beds made and items on desks put up.
4. Bathroom check with a quick toilet clean.
5. Dishes in sink put away.
6. Quickly sweep the kitchen and bathroom floors.
7. Pets removed or placed in a safe place for both them and the buyer's touring.

If you have children, and they are old enough to help, you can divide up the cleaning responsibilities to make sure they take ownership of their duty so that it is not all on you to keep the house clean. It is a great idea to have a leader for the day that will review everyone's quality of work and make the leader responsible for the overall cleanliness. Make it fun! Put on some music and a cheerful attitude and get it done. Motivate them with a long term reward for the entire family when you do get the house under contract, as well as a simple reward for them from time to time, like getting ice cream or going to see a movie.

Making a "tidy-up" schedule for the family is a great way to go about this. We all have busy lives, and sometimes leave the house at 7am and do not return until 7pm. Have a list of items that each family member does before bed, as well as another list prior to leaving in the morning. For example in the evening, it might be to put all laundry away and sweep floors. In the morning, one might wipe the counters down and be sure to make all the beds.

With pets, it is best to get them out of the house from the moment your house is active on the market to the time it goes under contract. Some buyers get leary when they see a few cats or dogs in the house as they worry about the damage they could have done or more commonly, how overwhelming the smells of the animals infiltrate the house. We all know cat pee is the worst! It can seep through the flooring and can stain the foundation to the point that it is almost impossible to remove. Those fur balls can be cute, but man, talk about a value killer.

If it is not possible to remove pets for the entire time showings are taking place, then figure out how to make sure your pets don't distract or worse, scare off a buyer. Place them in a crate in the laundry room where it will be cool, but still allow a buyer to feel safe from your pets. If you have a friendly neighbor, see if they will take them during the week incase you have a showing request. You can always take them on walks with you while the buyers have their appointment, but that can get pretty tiresome hanging out at the dog park all week. And the least desirable option, but sometimes the only option, is you can leave them in the backyard and not allow the buyers to go in the backyard for safety reasons. I don't love the last option because I want the buyers to be able to explore the home as much as possible, but sometimes it just can't be helped.

If you have a pet other than a dog or cat, I would highly suggest removing them. Snakes, lizards, turtles, and birds can really freak-out buyers and cause an instant negative emotional reaction that they may tie to the home and cause them to not even consider buying your house. Most people can look past it, but not all. Plus, if you are honest with yourself, they have a strong smell, especially ferrets.

Safety is my top priority with my clients that are occupying the house while selling. I always tell them, that if anyone says they were just driving in the neighborhood, and wanted to take a look to have them call me and set up a tour. I don't want to scare you with the horror stories that are passed around our office about a homeowner letting someone in their house for a quick look. Just don't do it. Even if someone says they saw your house previously and wanted to get a second tour. Refer them to your real estate professional. The agent representing the buyer on their tour of your home will be responsible for showing the house to help prevent any possible mischievous activity in addition to promoting all of the great features your house offers.

All prescription drugs, jewelry, firearms, and other valuables need to be removed or locked away in a safe place. If you have priceless collectables, such as art or sports memorabilia, don't leave it out and put away even before the pictures are taken. That's just too easy for a thief. Have items removed from the premises and safely stored.

Thankfully, I have never had any major incidents of items being stolen or injury caused to the homeowners. However, agents and buyers will leave doors unlocked (sometimes even open), lights on, tramp in mud, and a variety of other small but very uncourteous gestures. It happens, and sometimes the best way to prevent those from happening is to leave little notes throughout the house as reminders. Agents always forget if there is an alarm and if the homeowner wishes to keep it on during the listing timeframe. If you are choosing to keep your alarm set during the active period, be prepared, as it most certainly will be tripped.

In most markets, real estate professionals have an electronic lockbox that only licensed agents have access. So, every buyer's agent that tours with their client will have an electronic record of gaining access to your house. They are able to see who entered the house and when they left. If something did happen at the house, then your agent can go back and figure out when the event took place.

Running out of the house for each showing request is a hassle, I know, but it's so integral to the home selling process. Make sure that the house is in its best shape throughout the time showings are being held. You never know when your buyer will be touring. It will all be worth it in the end when you get that great offer.

ACTION STEPS

- Keep your house in top shape so that you impress all the buyers that tour.

- Decide what to do with pets.

- If you have kids, create a system for the family to work together to divide and conquer the cleaning responsibilities.

- Be safe, lock away valuables.

MARKET LIKE CRAZY
CHAPTER 9: GET THE WORD OUT

> *"Marketing is too important to be left to the marketing department."*
> *– David Packard*

NOW IT'S TIME TO MARKET your house like crazy. This is where your real estate professional gets to work on getting the word out to buyers and agents in the area. The goal here is to drive as much traffic to and through the house as possible. Yay! More showings!

Having your home in top condition with professional staging, top updates & features, HDR photography and a focus on what makes your product, *Cough, Cough*, your house different from the competition is really the best marketing strategy possible. Your house will be hitting 92% or more of the active buyers who are using the internet to find their new home. By using internet marketing we are meeting them where they are hanging out, and wowing them with an awesome product. Beautiful homes that are move-in-ready and stand out from the competition is what draw buyers in. However, we don't just settle at good enough.

STEP #9
MARKET LIKE CRAZY

This is the "X" factor when selling your house after price, condition and location have already been addressed. Every property is different and should be marketed uniquely depending on the location and the targeted buyer. With that said, I have some great marketing weapons in my arsenal for your real estate professional, as well as for yourself.

MULTIPLE LISTING SERVICE (MLS)

This is how your house ends up on Zillow, Realtor.com, Homes.com and the other hundreds of sites that display all the homes on the market in your area. It's great that buyers have more access to the active listings in the area and many times our buying clients know the active listings before we have had a chance to find them. The challenge for homeowners is still standing out from the thousands of homes available.

As discussed in the photography chapter, putting your best six pictures up front is a great idea along with selecting your first photo as something that catches the viewer's eye. Standing out enough for them to at least stop and see the rest of the pictures of your house. Another item neglected is the written description for buyers under the public remarks. Some real estate professionals are great and create helpful written details that entice, but also give a good overview of the house. Most do not, and it is actually quite frustrating having a potentially perfect buyer for a property to pass-over because there was little description on the home. All this can be avoided with just a little time, patience, and creativity to highlight the house's best features with descriptive words.

A well thought out description can stop the buyer just enough to explore your MLS website. Well thought out photo captions can overcome initial objections that may arise in a buyers mind. A well thought out written overview can persuade a buyer to set up a tour. Make sure you real estate professional is highlighting all the features of your house. That your agent is taking the time to do everything they can to make your house stand out from the competition.

Also, another item that real estate professionals often neglect is to not fill in all the applicable fields in the MLS. If the subdivision or location on the MLS map is set up incorrectly, many buyers searching through a "map draw" of their desired areas won't see your home. Same thing with popular items like a media room, pool, golf course community, the flooring and countertop types and so forth. Buyers with very specific search criteria may not see your house if all the applicable boxes are not selected. Be sure to give your agent thorough details of your house so your agent can fill in as many details as possible when it comes to listing on the MLS.

Just the other day, I was helping a new agent in our office with their first listing. They were going to skip through and not fill in all the available fields, and only do the mandatory ones. I advised them to take some time to do so. They did, and ended up negotiating a contract within four days. The buyers of the home only found the listing to begin with because of one of the obscure information fields, they had a specific preference in which direction the door faced. By this new agent taking the time to fill out these extra fields, they were able to quickly find the right buyers. Sometimes, more is more.

OPEN HOUSE

Who doesn't love walking through other people's homes to see their style, design and how they live? Well, I do at least and there are many buyers that do as well. The statistic we real estate professionals have been told is that only 1% of buyers who purchase any year

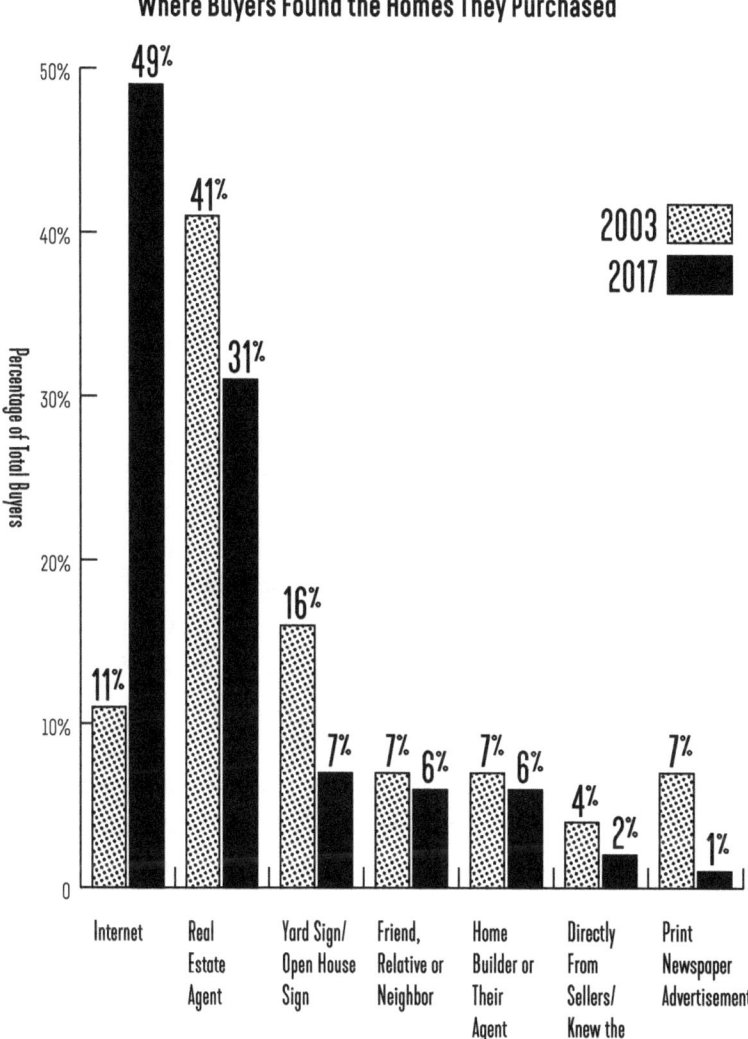

Figure 7

will find it through an open house. The National Association of Realtors® Profile[6] of a Home Buyer and Seller has the truth of the matter. Take a look at Figure 7 to see the reality of how home buyer will end up finding the home they purchase.

The top avenue is of course the Internet, #2 is the real estate professional and #3 is the open house or yard sign. I would have loved to have seen them split apart the yard sign and open house sign data but this report and chart are still helpful. It is fascinating that the yard sign/open house was 16% in 2003 and decreased consistently since then to 7%. I attribute this to technology. The amount of advances in photography and MLS systems alone has grown leaps and bounds since before 2003. You truly can get a good feel for a home by the pictures, and that just wasn't the case for our parents. In the past, physically touring the home was the only way.

I digress, the point is, open houses, yard signs, and tours are still important. Even at 7% it is much higher than the purported 1% urban legend stat. It is not uncommon for a buyer to be looking at homes online, see there is an Open House scheduled, visit the home and fall in love with it, all before contacting a real estate professional of their own. Or subsequently, be driving around a neighborhood on a Saturday, see an open house, and walk in for a visit.

Adding a few open houses could help to get the word out. More importantly, it will help you to reach that next largest chunk of buyers, and help you move on your merry way. Not all open houses are created equally, however. One open house tool I often use, is to list the house on the market and block all tours until the start of the first open house. This often creates a massive build up of interest. It is like a "Grand Opening Weekend" so to speak. Think about it. Your home is listed on Monday or Tuesday of that week and no tours are allowed until Saturday afternoon of the open house, do you think there might be a little build up of anticipation? Absolutely!

Also, remember that school of fish mentality? Think about going into an open house and hearing other buyers talk about how nice the house is and how they see themselves living in the home and enjoying the kitchen or the inviting patio. Don't you think that would help to validate the other buyers thoughts and feelings, and confirm to them that they should make an offer? It absolutely does!

Aside from the buyer's agent, there really is no (ethical) way of putting pressure on a buyer to make a purchase. When buyers normally tour a home, they usually set up a private tour so they are just bouncing their thoughts off of each other. With a busy open house, they are hearing other buyers share their thoughts and it motivates a buyer on the fence to get off and make an offer.

With this technique, I've had over 20 groups of buyers tour a house in less than two hours. The clients and I received three offers from the open house that same weekend. I've also had some that only had three groups total. However, overall, open houses can be an extremely effective tool.

The other thing about open houses is that it bumps your house to the top of many real estate websites so that more eyes are on your house. Those searching for open houses to tour that weekend will see your house, and are more likely to consider it even though it may be a different location than they have considered previously. Many times, buyers will be so interested that they set up a private tour with their real estate professional due to the extra marketing for the open house.

With the open house I will often run new social media ads, and target buyers in the area (more on social media later). I often send out postcards, drop off flyers and sometimes door knock, although people are pretty skittish about answering their front doors nowadays. Even if I can just get their attention for a moment, it is worth it, they may know a buyer that would be interested in moving into the neighborhood. It often occurs that homeowners will want their friends or family members to move to their amazing neighborhood and thus, you are tapping into a well of potential buyers.

I like to have fun with my open houses. I worked with a friend to create some hilarious open house signs; *"Never Flooded Except With Love"*, *"Your New Home Is Just Around The Corner"*, *"Uncle Jessie and Joey Are In the Basement"* (Full House anyone?) and my personal favorite, *"I Have Cookies!"* I usually bring cookies to my open houses, not because it makes them buy the house, but because it give me more time to pick their brain on the house. Doing so, I have more complete feedback to bring to the homeowners when we speak after the open house. I used to bake cookies for guests, but I kept burning the cookies because the oven would cook faster than what the package directed, so... burnt cookie smell was really awesome for the open house guests (sarcasm emphasised). It is right up there with burnt popcorn, or burnt toast. Anyway, it helps my open houses stand out and it gives the buyers a little laugh. Although, for the most part now, I just pick some up at a local bakery.

NEIGHBOR ONLY OPEN HOUSE

Another effective use of the open house is to do a "neighbors only" wine and cheese open house. This is a great way of stirring up some interest from your neighbors who may have friends or family that would like to move into the area. From figure 7, we saw that "friend, relative or neighbor" is tied for the 4th largest avenue buyers use to find a home.

In some neighborhoods or areas of the country, people just don't move. They have all of their family there, grow up there, go away for school and then end up coming back to buy a home in the same area. The National Association of Realtors® in 2018 national study[6] found that buyers move on average 12 miles away from their previous home. This means that even with all the buyers moving across state lines and to the opposite side of the country, it is still leveled out with people moving to a new house down the street from their last one.

People also want to have friends and family close to them, so using their natural tendency to play up the neighborhood to their loved ones is a great way to find a buyer for your house. Plus it is an excuse to have one last party with friends in the neighborhood before you move out.

TELL YOUR STORY

Check out the TED Talk, *"The Magical Science of Storytelling"* by David JP Phillips[3]. David opens his talk with a short story about a journalist, Rob Walker, who writes for the NY Times and wanted to test if storytelling truly is one of the most powerful tools in marketing. So, he purchased 200 items on ebay for a total of $129, most of them for less than $1. He then sent out emails to 200 different writers, authors, and journalists, asking them to create a story for the item he gave them. He then took the same items he purchased on eBay and added the story to it and listed them back on eBay and the results were astonishing. The sold total for the items was $8,000!

So, what's *your* story? What's the story of your house, your street, your neighborhood? Why did you enjoy living in the house so much? What major life events happened, and wonderful memories did you create? Share about how you love to sit in the backyard during the summer and enjoy grilling and watching the family play in a inflatable pool. Or how great the elementary school is that taught all your kids, especially one of them who had a reading challenge and was able to love reading from that point on. Share how "walkable" your house is to great restaurants, breweries, wine bars and the great times you had with friends. Share a short personal story that really tugs at the heart strings that buyers will then think, "that's what I really want in my new home." Just be sure to keep it a positive story.

Telling your story helps to change a house to a home. It allows the buyer to identify with the seller and their lifestyle and to desire that for themselves. People purchase things not necessarily for the item itself but for the feelings and perceived benefits it can provide them. People don't NEED the latest Mercedes model as their current car will get them from point A to B, but they buy it because it makes them feel significant. Think about what feelings your house can provide to the new owner.

A simple way to tell your story is to write it up on a piece of paper and leave on the kitchen counter or leave as an attachment on the MLS. A few pictures of the house decorated for Christmas or the family gathered around the dining room table for Thanksgiving can go a long way to evoke that emotion. If you have ever stayed in an AirBnB or a vacation rental property, they often have a guest book of memories. Sharing particular moments, or your part in your house's story, is like that. You can also create a little video testimonial sharing about your home and why you loved it so much.

SYNDICATE REAL ESTATE WEBSITES

As discussed earlier, your house will be posted on the Multiple Listing Service (MLS) and sent out to all syndicated websites that share real estate listings. Getting your house on the top of the most popular platforms is the best way to promote it where they are already spending time. It can be cost effective to promote your house as a "featured listing" or other similar tags to help it stand out from the competition.

Just like the MLS, it is a great idea to optimize the listing on the more popular platforms so they stand out. They change often but many times you can rank your listing higher with a walk through video from your phone or adding in more info. Anything you can do to add views will help to find your buyer.

SOCIAL MEDIA

With the increased use and sophistication of social media, targeted ads can be very effective with marketing your home to active buyers. Many platforms know which users are looking for homes and are most likely to move within the next couple of months, which is pretty amazing..and a little creepy, not gonna lie. Much less that they know how much income you make, your favorite websites, the number of eyelashes you have and the size of your most comfy underwear. They know more about you than the NSA. Because of this, it helps our marketing budget to go further by running ads to the active buyers who best fit the criteria of your house.

We can also target potential buyers geographically. Say you live out in the suburbs and you are looking to sell and move up to a larger house. We can target market your house's ad to your avatar and we also get creative and can find the buyer who doesn't live in the area but has a good chance to consider it.

In our market, for example, young families that live closer to downtown tend to buy their second home out in the suburbs. I see it all the time. Young professionals will buy or rent closer to downtown because that is where all their friends are living. Then they get married, have one kid, start thinking about schools and getting a bigger house so they move out to the "burbs". Remember that target buyer? It's not the buyer you WANT to buy your house, but the most PROBABLE buyer for your house.

Social Media Live Streams are great for open houses, as well as to do a simple video walk through with some creative commentary. Posting your listing on your social profiles is also a great idea to get your friends talking about your house and stirring up dormant buyers. When your real estate professional makes a social media post about your home, be sure to share it with your sphere of influence (your personal family and friends) as well.

CERTIFIED PRE-OWNED

When I say "certified pre-owned," what do you think?

Luxury cars, right? Using those words brings up emotions of next level of quality and extravagance. So, what if we could bring up those same feelings and emotions with a house?

Any house can be a "certified pre-owned home." All you need to do is have a professional inspector to come out to your house for an unbiased inspection. Then, take that inspection and get with a professional contractor to fix as many items on the report as possible. The final step is to hire an appraiser to independently appraise the house so you know its real value.

In our market, a seller is required to disclose any home inspection completed on the property within the last four years. So, take the inspection report and mark it up with all the repairs completed next to the corresponding items. If you fixed the furnace because it didn't have the correct fitting, then make a note of that to the side of the report. This will show proof and provide peace of mind to a buyer that they are not buying a money pit. Be sure to attach the contractors paid scope of work to the first page and post it to the MLS along with the appraisal. Make sure the paperwork is left on the counter in the kitchen along with "Certified Pre-Owned" signs to really stand out online, and when a buyer is touring multiple houses in one day. This is a fantastic tactic because it negates two of home buyer's biggest concerns; buying a money pit and over-paying.

This strategy is not for every home as it can cost a lot of money for the repairs; particularly large ticket repairs you may not have expected. It also could limit you with how much you can sell your house for if the appraiser is too safe with their evaluation. So, I don't recommend it for everyone, but it is a great marketing feature if you live in an older home surrounded by old houses. It may not make a huge difference if you live in a newer subdivision with brand new homes being built around you all the time, so talk with your real estate professional to see if this is the best strategy for you.

PROFESSIONAL WEBSITE (SEO)

Your house will basically have its own "website" on the MLS with all the pictures, features, attachments, and the virtual tour. However, it's great to have another website for more flexibility with marketing. With you own website you can run google ads, track a full array of metrics, email the link out to friends and family and get your house in front of a lot of people. It can be difficult to get great SEO rankings for a house on its own but I find it helpful as a landing page. Don't just create the website and expect other buyers to see it. Once the landing page is created, you will have to drive traffic to it through ads and social media posts. Otherwise, no one will see the page created translating into less views for the property. Most real estate professionals these days have a site of their own that they use to create landing pages and the like for their listings. They will walk you through all of this and easily set it up for you.

SIGN & RIDERS

A professional real estate sign is important to provide interest to neighbors and buyers driving around the neighborhood. I like to put out a rider that has the ability for buyers driving by to text a number to receive info and pictures straight to their phone. No more property flyer boxes with flyers littering your yard! I receive a notification and contact them as soon as possible to see if they would like to take a tour of the house. It is an effective way to break down any barriers a buyer may feel with requesting a tour.

Many times, I will put the yard sign up early to generate some interest with a "coming soon" sign rider. Or I will add additional riders that market its best feature like a "pool" or "newly remodeled." Previously, my area had a big flood affecting our market, so putting up "not flooded" riders was very helpful with easing buyer fears.

DIRECT MAIL

Direct mail isn't dead, it's just not the most effective means of marketing a house. While more expensive than many of the other marketing avenues, it can be very effective if used in the correct context. I like to do "Just Listed" postcards with many of my listings for 1,000 to 2,000 homes in the neighborhood. This is a great way generate some interest and provides another opportunity to get the neighbors telling their friends and family about your home.

A great use of direct mail is in conjunction with an event such as an open house or a neighborhood only wine and cheese open house. This meets some of the homeowners that may not take much notice to the happenings of real estate in the neighborhood. Remember the average distance a buyer moved in 2018 was 12 miles, so it is a good chance your buyer is close by.

AGENTS

Don't neglect having your agent work with other agents in their office and other local Realtors®. They may not have an active buyer, but they do have people in their database that may be dormant or they may know someone who wants to get in a particular area or to buy a home with a unique feature. Property e-blasts to all real estate professionals in the local area used to be an effective means of marking a house, but it seems like a majority of them get placed in the spam folder before anyone even sees them. At least that has been my experience.

Broker open houses used to be very popular tactics, as well. Now, broker open houses mostly feed agents who have no clients and not much else to do besides enjoying a free lunch. I will use them from time to time for agent feedback if a home is priced well, is in good condition, but just isn't receiving very many showings. It helps to elicit honest opinions from agents. That is the only effective means I have found in our market for a broker open house, but in your market it may be more effective.

I always chuckle a bit when a client forcefully requests a broker open house because they know it worked a long time ago when they first sold a house. With a little bit of education, I can help persuade them that if an agent really had a buyer looking in the area, they would more than likely set up a tour rather than wait for a broker open house. There are just more effective means of getting the house in front of buyers.

PRICE REDUCTIONS

You laugh but it is very effective. As the home sits on the market, it gets stale. Showings drop off, online traffic slows, and no decent offers come in. Drop the price! As we talked about in chapter 7, the new price could now be below a buyer's max price and show up in their search. It is amazing how the buyer traffic can increase even with just a modest price adjustment.

The longer a house is on the market, the more stale it gets. As we talked about previously, when buyers and agents see a house that is on the market longer than normal, they begin to wonder "what's wrong with the house?" Usually nothing other than it being overpriced for the condition and just needs a few price adjustments to get in to the fair market value. Homes that sit awhile with no price adjustments show buyers that a seller isn't willing to budge from their number and deters them from making offers. On the other hand, a few price drops during the listing period shows a buyer and their agent that a seller is willing to negotiate.

I have had sellers who were unwilling to budge from their high starting price. They tell me, "if someone wanted my house, they would put in an offer, even if it was low to start with." Investors are not afraid of submitting low offers, but MOST buyers who will pay the full market value don't want to insult a seller by submitting an offer that is even just 5% lower than the list price. They believe it will be insulting and a waste of time, so the logic of sticking with the starting price till death do you part, is a terrible idea.

FEEDBACK

Getting feedback is crazy important in selling a house. While it is not a proactive way to bring buyers in, it does help to adjust the price and condition based upon the feedback received. Both the buyers and the agent's feedback is important with getting into a buyers mind as to what they really think about your house. If feedback is consistently, "love the house but the wall colors were distracting." Then you can adjust the price or provide a credit at closing so the paint color of the walls is no longer a sticking point for the buyer to do the repair themselves.

Feedback is so important that I will call, email and text agents multiple times to get their buyers opinion of the home. My feedback rate shoots up to around 80% which helps to keep the sellers out of the dark. I also communicate every Tuesday with every seller all of the showing feedback, marketing activities and will update them on any activity in the neighborhood. This keeps communication open and everyone in the loop.

MARKETING SCHEDULE

Marketing a house is the process of preparing and optimizing it for the most likely buyer. Then it is about getting the word out. I like to use a marketing schedule that plans out the activities and promotions to help keep the house as fresh as possible and the traffic flowing in. The first week on the market has the biggest push. This is when your listing is the hot and new product on the market.

Plan out the open houses as best as possible to coincide with social media campaigns leading up to each event in order to drive as much traffic to the listing as possible. Another great idea is to build in price adjustments within the marketing calendar. This will allow you, the homeowner, to know when to expect them. It is not a firm event that you have to drop the price, but it allows for the discussion. It is also helpful to review the average number of showings other homes in a similar price range are receiving, and compare with your house.

If the average number of showings is 15 per month and the listing is only at 3, then it is time to realistically assess why. More often than not, the house is overpriced. To review a sample marketing calendar, check out TheRealEstateGamePlan.com along with the bonus article, "The Best Inexpensive Updates & Repairs to Do Prior to Selling Your Home."

WRAP UP

As agents, we joke that the non-dynamic (a nice way of saying lazy or cheap) agents will do the triple "P". **P**lace a sign in the yard, **P**ut it on the MLS and **P**ray that it sells. I'm all about prayer, but your real estate professional needs to do better than just the minimal amount of marketing. Work with a top professional that will help you correctly position the house for sale and will then will market it like crazy.

ACTION PLAN

- Create a marketing plan with your real estate professional to get your house in front of as many buyers as possible.

- Not all of these marketing tactics may be right for your house, so select the ones that fit best with your overall game plan.

THE PROCESS
CHAPTER 10: ACCEPT THE RIGHT OFFER

*"ABC. 'A', always. 'B', be. 'C', closing.
Always be closing!"*
– Blake (in Glengarry Glen Ross)

A T THIS POINT, YOUR HOUSE IS ON THE MARKET, you have done the exhausting pre-listing work, marketed it like crazy, made the house available as much as possible, and suddenly you get an offer. Hold on cowboy, don't go accepting the first offer right away. This chapter will focus on the process of accepting the right offer and moving toward closing. Each state is different with their laws and practices so understand there will be some differences. This chapter will, however, provide decent framework for the general steps to closing along with brilliant tips and tricks.

You have an offer in, now you will need to thoroughly review the contract offer and vet the buyer. First, look at the big items; offer price, financing, closing date, seller concessions and repair requests. Usually, if a buyer is too far off on the big items then negotiating the small, but very important terms, is a waste of time. With the offer price, check to see how much the buyer is putting down. Usually, the higher the down payment the better. Check to see what kind of financing they are applying for from the lender's pre-approval letter. The major types of loans are Conventional, FHA (Federal Housing Administration), VA (Veterans Affairs), and the USDA (United States Department of Agriculture, why do they do loans? I have no idea...they could have definitely put it under the FHA and added a rural loan but that's just my 2 cents).

Each of the major loans have different advantages and disadvantages for the buyer but as the seller, you will need to know which ones will affect you the most and how. The VA has expenses that the veteran is unable to pay for, like a pest inspection (in specific areas of the United States), certain closing costs and their buying broker's fees. Both the VA and FHA (conventional to some extent) have a variety of requirements that the house is safe, sound and sanitary. The VA will also send their own inspector to inspect the house in addition to the buyer hiring a private inspector (in some states this is required).

In addition, different loans provide the option of varying seller concessions. A seller concession is when a seller provides a discount on the sale price to levitate some of the closing costs. For example, a buyer may offer $300,000 with a conventional loan but ask for $9,000 in concessions, which leaves you at a $291,000 net offer price. When an FHA or VA buyer puts the least amount of money down (VA is 0% down) and asks for the max in concessions, I get worried because if something else comes up with the house, or if the buyer's credit score changes a little, or they don't quite have enough cash in reserve, it could prevent them from closing. I have closed many homes with buyers in that position, so it doesn't mean they are necessarily untrustworthy, but it does mean that a conventional buyer with 20% down and no seller concessions is more likely a stronger buyer, and less likely to back out due to loan approval issues.

I almost always talk with the lender about the credit and financial ability of the buyer. The lender is unable to give me specifics, but they will generally share their thoughts on the buyers overall picture. Looking at the type of loan, down payment, concession request, and the discussion with with the lender will give you a better idea of how strong the buyer is.

After looking at the more important terms of the contract, talk with your real estate professional about the other costs and contingencies you should be worried about. Your professional can create an "estimated net sheet," which is a simple calculation of the closing costs and what you can expect to "net" on the sale of the house at that price.

Respond to the buyer with a counter of price and terms. In a hot market, you may not need to drop the price much or give too favorable terms to the buyer. So make sure you are aware of your city's market, and then your neighborhood's market as they can be very different. Also, when responding, make sure that you don't convey any form of acceptance to the offer unless you decide to accept it. Here in Texas, if we send an email saying, "the seller will accept $292,000 with..." even if we do not have a signed contract, it is considered a communication of acceptance and could get you in major trouble if you do not accept it. I always say, "the seller would prefer" or "a more favorable offer would..." when countering an offer. So, just be careful.

As discussed previously, homes in the U.S. have historically sold for 97% of the list price. That means there is usually a little wiggle room in negotiations, so don't be hurt if a buyer comes in lower than your listing price. It is common to negotiate back and forth a few times to iron out the details for the best possible agreement.

If you have multiple offers on your house, then talk with your agent as to how to best proceed. In Texas, we don't have escalation clauses that automatically bump the sales price up if the seller accepts a higher one as a back-up offer, but maybe your state does. Have your professional share with you the best practices and what to expect.

With multiple offers, I usually ask for each buyers "highest and best" offer and they are invited to re-submit their best offer blindly. Once an offer is accepted and executed, the seller has little recourse to back out of the contract and can only negotiate with the accepted buyer (some states vary). So, I make sure that I clearly explain that there is no backing out, or deciding not to move once they have accepted an offer. If they decided not to sell the house, they could be sued, taken to court and forced to sell at the agreed upon terms. Court, is never fun. So, step #10 is immensely important:

STEP #10:
ACCEPT THE RIGHT OFFER

    Just because an offer is higher than all the others doesn't necessarily mean it is the best for you. I have already discussed the concerns about financing, but maybe the closing date is really important, or that you need to close on the house and lease it back for a little while so you can apply the proceeds to the purchase of your new house. Whatever it is, negotiate to get as much as you reasonably can, and make sure you get the terms that are most important to you.

DEPOSITING EARNEST & OPTION MONEY

Once a contract is signed, there is usually some form of compensation given to the seller to show that the buyer is earnest about purchasing their house. In our market it is called Earnest Money and Option Money. The Option Money goes towards the Option Period, which is when a buyer has the unrestricted right to backout of the contract for any reason. This is usually when the inspection and other repair quotes are gathered by the purchaser. The amount given for Option Money is negotiable, but it is usually a couple hundred dollars and can go toward the closing costs if the buyer moves forward. If the buyer backs out, then the seller keeps the Option Money.

The Earnest Money is negotiable as well (like many things in real estate) and tends to be 1% to 2% of the purchase price. This money is held in an escrow account at the title company (your state may be different). This is the money that tells the seller that the buyer is "earnest" about their intent to purchase the house. If a buyer backs out during the Option Period, typically because both parties cannot agree on concessions or repairs identified after inspections, then typically the Earnest Money is returned to the buyer. If a buyer backs out of the contract outside of their contingencies, then the earnest money usually goes to the seller. Talk with your real estate professional or attorney as there are usually multiple contingencies in a contract. This is always a big point of contention and can get real ugly, real quick. Especially if one party objects to which side should receive the earnest money.

Both the Earnest & Option Money checks need to be received within a set amount of time or the buyer risks losing their right to back out for any reason during the Option Period (inspection period).

INSPECTION PERIOD (OPTION PERIOD)

The next step is for the buyer to perform their own inspections on the house with a third-party inspector. If they use a second cousin who is just a handy guy, you may not want to take his word with any of his findings. Most buyers will use a state licensed inspector. Be aware that the inspector will always find something wrong with your house. Property code changes about every week, and even new houses don't always meet code 100%. A resale home will most likely not meet the newest code and many times will be grandfathered in from having to comply. However, there may be some items so outdated, or in need of repair, that they are a safety concern for the new buyer.

When we purchased our first home it was sold as a foreclosure. After closing, we did an extensive remodel because it just was not livable. We didn't realize it at purchase, but the house did not have ground wiring in it (just two prong outlets instead of the normal three). Our home was built in 1971, at that time it was not code to have a ground. We had to spend extra money to get it up to code, but it was worth it for the peace of mind. Not to mention the fact that the walls were already open, so the perfect time to get work done.

Whether an inspector or a trade is going to be at the house, the buyer's agent needs to schedule it and inform you of the people that will be in the house incase anything happens. Make sure you get the full contact info of every visitor as you have a right to know who is coming into your house.

The buyer will most likely want items that are a safety concern addressed in addition to as much as they can squeeze out of you. In my experience, most sellers negotiate between $500 and $1,500 in concessions during the Option Period. If the buyer did not hit you hard on price in the up front negotiations, they usually try to make it up during the Option Period after they have some educated ammo with the inspection report.

After receiving the inspection report, the buyer usually asks for a ridiculous amount of repairs or compensation in the form of a price drop or concessions. This is usually just them testing the waters and I usually suggest to respond with a low counter. The reason is that we don't know what items are more important to the buyer. They could have 20 items on the report that they say they are concerned with, but after our counter, they usually come back and say, "well, we at least have to have the roof repairs, faucet leak and the air conditioning serviced" or whatever their top concerns are. Now that is something you can work with!

I always recommend giving a concession versus having the repairs done by the seller. The reason is that the quality of work will never be done up to the standard that the buyer desires. It is a hassle to spend money for the inspector and other trades to come back out to verify the proper completion. Also, if you agree to do the repairs, you have to have a professional contractor or trade to get the work completed as doing the work yourself could open you up to a huge liability. Not to mention, the buyer will always think you did a subpar job. How are they to know you apprenticed under Chip Gains for 10 years, and have built a cabin in the woods with your own two hands?

I made this mistake during my second year in real estate. I was helping my good friend who is a general contractor sell his house and after we received the inspection report, we just had his sub-contractors do the work. When the buyers were informed they were livid. I had long conversations with the agent about the repairs, and they sent trade after trade to verify it was done correctly. At one point we were scheduled to meet with the buyer's agent and do a walk-through at the house. I arrived just a little late, and the buyer's agent and my clients were literally in a screaming match in the kitchen. I was able to talk each side down and negotiate an agreeable solution for both sides for just a couple hundred dollars. It was a tremendous learning experience, and I never want to repeat that again. Take it from me, it's not worth it.

So, make it easy on yourself, and give the buyer a concession to handle the repairs themselves after closing.

Sometimes it is unavoidable as repairs are required by the lender or insurance underwriter. In Texas, you cannot get home insurance if a house has an overlay roof. An overlay roof is when a roof was not removed prior to the roofer adding a new roof. Whether it's two, four, or more roofs on one house, it puts a tremendous stress on the support and foundation that it was not designed for and can cause tremendous damage. Thankfully, it is not a common practice anymore and would only be something you would really look for in an older home.

I once toured a house that had four overlay roofs on it! Needless to say, it would have been a large expense, but necessary for a seller to have corrected. Otherwise, the buyer would not have been able to get approved for a loan on the house (cash is no problem). Talk with your professional to discuss any other big repair items that could possibly prevent the sale of your house.

Okay, back to negotiating. After back and forth a few times during the Option Period, most buyers who really want the house will work out an agreeable solution. If not, then the house goes back on the market.

APPRAISAL & SURVEY

If the buyer moves forward and is financing the purchase, then the lender will require an appraisal and a survey. The appraisal, as we have discussed before, is done by a third-party appraiser who is making sure the bank is not lending on a house that is over the amount of the market value. If it is higher, in their eyes at least, than the market value, you may have to drop your price to sell. Check out chapter 7 on pricing to get a better idea of the options you have if the price is low. If the appraised value meets or exceeds the accepted price, then the buyer is able to move forward. Unfortunately, you won't be able to raise the price if the appraisal is higher than your contract price.

The survey is done by a surveyor and the survey tells the bank, and the buyer, if the house and all of the permanent structures sit within the boundary lines of the property according to the local Tax Record. It will show the utility easements, property lines, aerial easements, encroachments and so forth. Many times, the fence will be off the property line a little but it usually isn't enough to warrant any concern by the buyer's underwriter or the title company. You should get worried when the title company is concerned about anything on the survey. This is typically a sign of a major issue that can stop a sale in its tracks.

One client of mine purchased a home in which a part of the garage and the steps to the garage apartment were encroaching on the neighbor's property. Luckily, the owner of the other property had given a previous seller a variance for it and they were able to get the loan to purchase the house without any issue. It worked out in that instance, but could have not only killed the deal for my buyer, but have been an issue for the seller as well.

OTHER CONTINGENCIES

The fewer contingencies in your contract the better. The definition of a contingency is the dependence on chance or on the fulfillment of a condition. There are a multitude of contingencies in a contract, depending upon how it is written up. Here, I want to review some of the more standard contingencies.

One really important contingency is the "Third Party Financing Contingency" that allows the buyer to back out if they are unable to get loan approval within a certain time. This is peace of mind for the buyer to not have to lose their earnest money should something come up with their finances or their credit report. This is a huge contingency for a seller and I recommend negotiating the time period for this contingency to as low as reasonably possible.

"Contingency of the Sale of Another Property" happens when a buyer needs to sell their current house and get the proceeds to put down toward the purchase of your house. Although extremely common, this is even more risky because you are at the mercy of your buyer's buyer being able to qualify for their loan and close on time so your buyer can purchase your house (and then you purchase your new home). It can be a domino train wreck if one party is not able to close. With that said, if a house hasn't had any offers and a strong offer with a "Contingency of the Sale of Another Property" comes in, then I would strongly consider it and make the sellers aware of the uncertainty that may come with it. I have closed many homes in this situation, and many of them have been smooth, easy closings while only a small percentage have had to backout from their other home not selling.

If a house is in a Homeowners Association (HOA), there is always an HOA contingency unless otherwise agreed upon. A buyer needs to make sure a seller is in good standing with the HOA with no unpaid dues or fines. Most HOA's have the power to foreclose on a homeowner, so the transaction attorney or escrow officer will do the necessary due diligence to make sure none of the above are issues. Also, make sure to read the language in the HOA section carefully as a buyer may have the option to back out and receive their earnest money back if the HOA rules and bylaws are not submitted to them within a specific timeframe. This HOA contingency effects not just single family homes in the suburbs, but condo and townhome communities as well.

There are a variety of other addendum and contingencies to discuss with your real estate professional from "Lead Based Paint," to "Wetlands Protection," to bedbugs and radon gas. There are a myriad of contingencies that are often time sensitive, so stay on top of all the important deadlines. The worst thing that could happen is for you to get close to closing, and the buyer backs out and receives their earnest money back because of some small clause in the real estate contract.

CLOSING

Finally we are getting to the fun part, moving! After most of the contingencies have been satisfied, you will need to pack and get everything out of the house prior to closing. Owners need to vacate the property the day before closing so the buyer can do the final walk through and take over the property after the funds have been received. If you need more time, you can negotiate with the buyer to lease the property from them. Usually, this occurs so the funds will be received and sent for the purchase of your new house so you don't have to do a double move. No one likes moving, not even professional movers.

Leasing back from the buyer, now the new owner, changes the relationship from buyer & seller to tenant & landlord. You may have to do a full lease application and put down a deposit like a normal renter, not to mention getting renters insurance. Be sure to talk with your insurance professional because a major catastrophe may not be covered with your previous homeowners insurance and then you end up in a court battle with the new owner for who is responsible for the damages.

If you are not getting a lease from the new owner to stay in the house a little longer, then make sure that everything thing you want to take is out of the house prior to closing. Anything left in the house, (including your contractor's power washer that was left in the garage and who never returned your calls) is now the property of the new owner. If you negotiated for the buyer to keep the non-realty items (anything that isn't attached permanently such as the washer, dryer, and refrigerator), then don't be a cheapskate and take it. Even if you feel like it is retribution for a sour negotiating experience, you need to comply with the contract. You are legally bound to the contract you and the buyers agreed to.

The buyer will normally do a walk-through 24 hours prior to closing to make sure the house is in order. If you can, have the house professionally cleaned or at least swept and cleaned up as it would be strange for you to rent a vacation house and the owner not have it cleaned prior to your reservation.

Finally, make sure to keep the utilities on until at least the day of closing. If they shut off the utilities, then the providers will charge the buyer extra fees to turn them back on. So, as a courteous act, keep them on a day or so longer.

After working through the Option Period and getting a winning appraisal, most of the transaction is downhill and often glides into a smooth closing. Things pop up from time to time, as every real estate transaction is unique, so make sure to protect yourself by staying on top of all the important dates in the contract and disclosing any required information.

ACTION STEPS

- Thoroughly vet your buyer's offer and make sure to select the right one.

- Know the important dates in the contract to stay in compliance and reduce the likelihood of the buyer backing out without giving you compensation.

- Reduce the contingencies and steer them to favorable terms as much as possible.

- Be open to negotiating after the inspection and drill down to the buyers "must haves."

THE WRAP UP
THAT'S ALL FOLKS

"Opportunities come infrequently. When it rains gold, put out the bucket, not the thimble"
– Warren Buffet

THE PURPOSE OF THIS BOOK is to provide you with a step by step framework for assessing and addressing the aspects of selling your house to achieve max profit. I wish all of the clients I have been able to assist over the years knew this information before they began their real estate journeys. Homes that languished needlessly on the market from being overpriced and not correctly updated would have been prevented, more times that not. Following this game plan would have helped relieve the burdensome holding costs or stressful double mortgage payments carried by some.

My wish is that all sellers, my own clients, or another real estate professionals, took the time to think of their end buyer before adding any updates. I wish that anyone desiring to sell their home, took the time to fully assess their house and create a game plan rather than calling on me, or their agent, to request their home on the market as soon as possible without fully preparing to ensure the greatest success.

Thankfully, I don't have to wish for a better experience for you. While I can't guarantee a quick sale for boat loads of cash, I do know that your preparation, simply by reading through this book, will set you miles ahead of your competition. That following the steps outlined within this book, creating your game plan, working with the right professionals, and making adjustments as needed, will allow your house to stand out. All of this to help with your overall goal of quickly selling your home, and for the highest profit possible. After all, who doesn't like max profit?

All the Best,

Paul Holub
Keller Williams Realty
paulholub.com

REFERENCES

1. "Cost vs Value Report of 2018." Remodeling.hw.net, 2018, www.remodeling.hw.net/cost-vs-value/2018/.

2. Kuhn, George. "How Market Research Saved Febreze | Consumer Behavior Case Study." Market Research Company | Drive Research, Market Research Company | Drive Research, 18 Jan. 2017, www.driveresearch.com/single-post/2016/11/03/How-Market-Research-Saved-Febreze-Consumer-Behavior-Case-Study.

3. Phillips, David JD. "The Magical Science of Storytelling." TED Talks-Stockholm 2015. TED Talks, 2015, Stockholm, www.youtube.com/watch?v=Nj-hdQMa3uA.

4. Quint, Rose. "Housing Preferences across Generations (Part I)." Eye On Housing, 25 Apr. 2016, eyeonhousing.org/2016/03/housing-preferences-across-generations-part-i/.

5. Sipola, Chris. "The Price of Overpricing: How Listing Price Impacts Time on Market - Zillow Research." Premier Agent Resource Center, Zillow, 21 Nov. 2017, www.zillow.com/research/overpricing-impacts-time-market-12476/.

6. Yun, Lawrence, et al. 2017 Profile of Home Buyers and Sellers. National Association of Realtors, 2017, pp. 1–144, 2017 Profile of Home Buyers and Sellers, www.nar.realtor/sites/default/files/documents/2017-profile-of-home-buyers-and-sellers-11-20-2017.pdf.

HOME STAGING CHECKLIST

This is a checklist of the major items to address and to do prior to going 'active' on the market. This task list will help you do a basic staging job on your house and is great for tackling prior to meeting with your professional stager.

ESSENTIAL HOME ITEMS

- Deep clean carpet, polish wood flooring and mega scrub all tile flooring (magic eraser is amazing).

- Patch holes and provide touch up paint or fresh paint throughout the house.

- Wall and ceiling texture should be consistent, particularly where patches have been made. If it is distracting, have a professional address.

- Address any water stains, wall cracks or other issues that could cause great concern for the buyer.

- Deep clean bathrooms and the kitchen.

- Wipe all baseboards and polish woodwork.

- Clean fan blades.

- Remove all family photos, magazines, incense, trophies and religious items.

- Pack up personal collectables and other unique pieces that could be a distraction to the buyer.

- Eliminate any and all odors.

- Clean light switches and switch plates, lamp shades

(should not have plastic covering) and be sure all light bulbs are working and do not need to be replaced.

- Replace air filters and wipe down air grates.
- NEVER place a rug over carpet, it appears as if the owner is hiding something underneath (which is 100% the case).

ENTRY

- Remove family pictures and replace with art or inspirational quotes.
- Declutter entryway walls.
- Remove shoe and coat racks.

CURB APPEAL

- Power Wash sidewalks, driveway and the house if needed (check to make sure what the setting is before starting on the house, so you don't damage the siding).
- Add black or natural colored mulch to the flower beds along with fresh annuals.
- Keep flower beds weeded.
- Trim bushes and trees to show the beauty of the house.
- Have yard neatly trimmed, mowed, and fertilized.
- The Doormat should be new or in good condition.
- Front door should be newly stained or painted for best results.
- House number should be visible.

DINING ROOM

- Clear off table and chairs (no bills or homework).

- Brass fixtures made before 1990 should all be updated to a consistent and modern style.

- Remove tablecloth (unless table is dingy).

- Add a simple and timeless centerpiece (a runner with a bowl of lemons is classic but use some creativity).

- Take dining room table leaf out for 4 chairs instead of 6.

STUDY OR OFFICE

- Remove any personal information such as bank account info, tax returns or confidential information.

- Declutter office desk to the bare essentials: computer, lamp, printer (if you can't hide below the desk or in a cabinet) and maybe an art piece or two.

- Remove personal or family pictures.

- Hide or remove files that are outside of cabinets.

- Declutter bookshelf with fewer books and removing any "controversial" ones.

LIVING ROOM

- Hide technology: remotes, cable boxes, cords, speakers, etc.

- Position furniture to the most inviting layout and not necessarily the best TV watching.

- Remove surplus furniture.

- Clean fireplace and add new logs if wood burning.
- Mantle should have hooks and nails removed along with all personal photos.
- Coffee table should be clear of everything except for an accent piece: candles, decorative bowl, interesting book.
- Blinds should be open as much as possible to indirect

  light and dark solar screens removed.

KITCHEN

- Fully remove everything off the countertops: coffee pot, towels, soap, small appliances, etc.
- Remove non-essential items from cabinets to allow for more space.
- Clean cabinets, repair scratches, updated cabinet pulls (if necessary) and remove items such as plants from the top of the cabinets.
- Clear off the refrigerator (no magnets or pictures).
- Trash can should be hidden.
- Deep clean grout lines, all appliances, behind refrigerator and wipe down all pantry shelves.
- Check that the countertop seam between the backsplash is properly caulked along with sink and other required locations.

MASTER BEDROOM

- Remove excess furniture.
- Night stands should be free from all clutter.
- Remove exercise equipment.
- Leave out your best throw pillows and bedspread (or purchase new).

BATHROOMS

- Remove all items from countertops and store away.
- Toilets, bathtub, and shower surround should all be scrubbed clean and free of mildew.

CLOSETS

- The master closet is the most important and should be decluttered and left with only essentials.
- A few wrapped gift bags throughout in a particular color really compliments the space.
- Secondary bedrooms should be decluttered if possible (pre-pack).

BACKYARD

- Face patio furniture toward the house.
- Add colorful throw pillows and centerpiece for table.
- Pick up pet mess.

- Remove trampoline and other yard clutter.

Staging distracts a buyer from focusing on any minor defects in the house and seeing the beauty of the entire home. Most people do not have a vision for what the house can look like with their things in it, so staging helps to provide the visual for the buyers.

Contributions provided by Hillary Roy with Room Redezign

RESOURCES Supplemental Materials | **153**

Sign up at

Realestategameplan.com

for the list of

"The Best Inexpensive Updates & Repairs to Do Prior to Selling Your Home"

and an example

"Real Estate Game Plan Marketing Calendar."

www.ingramcontent.com/pod-product-compliance
Lightning Source LLC
Chambersburg PA
CBHW070543090426
42735CB00013B/3058